国家留学基金(留金法[2011]5024号)资助
成都理工大学中青年科研骨干教师培养计划(KYGG201313)资助
四川省旅游业青年专家培养计划资助

 21世纪全国高等院校旅游管理类创新型应用人才培养规划教材

英语导游实务

Essentials for English-Speaking Tourist Guide: Theory and Practice

唐勇 编著

内 容 简 介

英语导游实务是旅游管理、酒店管理、会展与服务管理等专业的核心课程。本书致力于培养学生的英语导游服务与业务实践能力。本书可作为教材，也可作为英语导游的工作用书，将帮助学生较全面地了解并掌握英文导游员在带团过程中的业务流程、实务技能、必备知识等，为立志于考取国家旅游局导游资格证书的学生提供专业、系统、有效的指导和帮助。

本书的内容体系立足于国内导游证考试大纲及国外导游培训与考核标准，及时反映旅游及导游行业实践及动态，重点在导游英语专业词汇学习、导游词撰写、导游翻译练习（口笔译）方面有所突破，将知识习得、技能与能力培育融入教材内容中。主要包括如下内容：导游的历史、现状与未来，导游人员，导游工作内容，导游语言艺术，旅游事故的预防和处理，旅行和交际常识等。本书邀请外国专家审定了全书的英文部分，确保了语言的规范性、可读性及实用性。

图书在版编目(CIP)数据

英语导游实务/唐勇编著. —北京：北京大学出版社，2013.9
(21世纪全国高等院校旅游管理类创新型应用人才培养规划教材)
ISBN 978-7-301-22986-6

Ⅰ. ①英… Ⅱ. ①唐… Ⅲ. ①导游—英语—高等学校—教材 Ⅳ. ①H31

中国版本图书馆 CIP 数据核字(2013)第 182815 号

书　　　　名：	英语导游实务
著作责任者：	唐　勇　编著
策 划 编 辑：	莫　愚
责 任 编 辑：	莫　愚
标 准 书 号：	ISBN 978-7-301-22986-6/C·0928
出 版 发 行：	北京大学出版社
地　　　　址：	北京市海淀区成府路 205 号　100871
网　　　　址：	http://www.pup.cn　新浪官方微博：@北京大学出版社
电 子 信 箱：	pup_6@163.com
电　　　　话：	邮购部 62752015　发行部 62750672　编辑部 62750667　出版部 62754962
印　刷　者：	三河市北燕印装有限公司
经　销　者：	新华书店
	787 毫米×1092 毫米　16 开本　16.25 印张　390 千字
	2013 年 9 月第 1 版　2015 年 5 月第 2 次印刷
定　　　　价：	33.00 元

未经许可，不得以任何方式复制或抄袭本书之部分或全部内容。
版权所有，侵权必究
举报电话：010-62752024　电子信箱：fd@pup.pku.edu.cn

编写人员名单

唐　勇　成都理工大学旅游与城乡规划学院
曾祥裕　四川大学南亚研究所
秦宏瑶　四川大学旅游学院
钟　洁　西南民族大学历史旅游学院
陆雪姗　四川大学锦城学院
崔佳春　成都理工大学旅游与城乡规划学院
陈　兴　成都理工大学旅游与城乡规划学院
余志勇　成都理工大学旅游与城乡规划学院
董　海　成都市导游服务公司

前言

随着旅游业的全面发展，政府、高校和导游行业都越来越重视导游业务的教学与培训，各类导游业务培训教材也大量上市。但现有导游培训教材还有一定的盲区。例如，大部分导游业务的图书均为汉语，而英文的导游读物又主要侧重于导游词撰写等。概言之，目前我国尚欠缺一部全面介绍导游业务的英文教材。

本书第一章为导论，介绍了本书编写目的、主要内容、编排体例、学习进度建议等。第二章为导游史话，介绍了导游职业的历史、现状与未来。第三章为导游概说，主要介绍导游人员的类型及主要工作内容等。第四章主要讨论了国内外对导游的考核与培训，重点介绍了我国的导游资格考试、年检制度等，实用性较强。第五章向读者介绍了规范管理导游行为的政策法规，是未来导游执业者的必读章节。第六章详细介绍了导游业务流程，是本书的一大重点。第七章探讨带团流程，侧重导游实务。第八章、第九章、第十章分别为讲解技巧、沟通技巧和团队管理，具体涉及导游语言艺术、旅游事故的预防和处理、交际与沟通技巧、时间管理等内容，具有重要参考价值。

本书的特色主要体现在四个方面。

第一，本书为英文为主、中文为辅的创新教材，其编写借鉴了国外教材的成功经验，同时参考了国内较成熟的做法，并结合了编者在相关教学活动与导游实践中的具体思考，兼具国际视野和严谨学理。

第二，本书用英语较全面地介绍了英文导游业务的主要流程，弥补了英文导游业务教材的空白，旨在帮助读者以中英双语特别是英语熟悉导游业务，并为其进一步借鉴国际经验建立必要基础。

第三，本书体例较完备，知识面较为开阔。本书以导游业务为主干，编排了导游知识、国际旅游组织概况、国家政策法规、导游实训案例、中国文化常识、中国历史概况等内容，具有较强的知识性，很多内容可直接用于组织导游词。

第四，本书特别注意帮助读者获得执业资格。为此，编者精心设计试题，特别侧重中高级英语导游考试的实战练习，为有意考取国家旅游局导游资格证书的学生提供专业、系统、有效的指导和帮助。

综上，本书最大的特点是帮助学生在学理、业务、国际视野、执业资格能力上获得全面提升。

本书的编写参阅了大量的中英文教材、专著和论文，在此谨向作者表示衷心感谢！北京大学出版社为本书出版提供了极为宝贵的支持，在此一并致谢。

本书是英语导游业务教材上的一次全新尝试，编者水平有限，时间紧凑，不足之处在所难免，敬请广大读者批评指正，以利于本书的修订完善。对读者惠赐意见，编者特预致谢忱！

编　者
2013 年 8 月

Preface

In recent decades, there has been a considerable increase in the number of training manuals for tourist guide on the market. However, those works with insufficiont attention to the growing literature outside of China make us determined in our research.

In traditional Chinese philosophy, there is always a tension between "knowing" versus "doing". To achieve this, the author should, as a Chinese expression says, "have one's knowledge integrated to one's doing". As both teachers and professionals in the field of tourism studies, we are striving to fulfill our duty. In this book, we intend to write about the essential knowledge and skills for an English-speaking tourist guide, not in Chinese, but in English. Textbooks of this kind should not simply be a translation work of its Chinese version, or selection of works in English. It should be a picture completing itself, rather than an inventory of names in the literature.

In his preface to *Fortress Besieged*, CH'IEN Chung-Shu states,"while he was writing his book, it was a time of great grief and disruption, during which he thought several times of giving up, and he was to finish the book through the accumulation of many small moments". If the great man's deep sorrow contributes to his masterpiece, our idleness inspires us to put bits and ends, or ideas, thoughts and experiences together to write this book. This book is the result of many long hours and the dedication of many people, taking about three years to collate. It is quite an interesting and challenging task. In preparing this work, we had tried to use our judgment in selecting what we considered important and relevant from a variety of interdisciplinary sources. Thanks to the time we spent writing and referencing from volumes of books, papers and sources either in Chinese or in English, we finally finished it. Primarily, this book aims to assist our students as a tourist guide training course in English. Catering to this intention, we tried to use a succinct and simple English to write. We hope we have succeeded.

We are very excited about writing this book, and hope it will add to the valuable collection in the discipline as first of its kind helping students equipped with global vision. This book serves no more than an introduction to the fundamental knowledge and basic skills in tour guiding. If the reader wishes to learn more about this subject, we would suggest him or her referring to the bibliography listed in this book.

This work is supported by the China Scholarship Council, the Key Teachers Development Fellowship for Scientific Research at Chengdu University of Technology (CDUT), and the Fellowship for Early Career Faculty in Tourism Science by Sichuan Tourism Adminstration. We are grateful to the support, while noting that they are not responsible for the views expressed here. We would like to thank students from the Dept. of Tourism Development and Management, College of Tourism and Urban-rural Planning, CDUT, for their most helpful comments on earlier drafts of the book. Our sincere thanks also goes to Mr. Jean Vuillemain, lecturer from the collaborative Education Programme between Edge Hill University and CDUT, and Sarah Tynen from University of Colorado at boulder who proofread the work and make it more readable while Mr. Mo Yu from Peking University Press provides us with great suggestions.

As the saying goes,"tourism knows no border and life is a journey for us to explore". Wish you a successful professional career in tour guiding!

Contents 目录

Chapter 1	Introduction to the Course	0
	1.1 Textbook at a Glance	2
	1.2 Structure of Each Chapter	4
	1.3 Level of the Textbook	5
	1.4 Course Structure	5
	1.5 Teaching and Learning Strategies	6
	1.6 Assessment Details	6
	1.7 Teaching Plan	7
Chapter 2	Tour Guiding: Its Origin, Growth and Future	14
	2.1 Beginning of the Story	17
	2.2 Development of the Story	19
	2.3 Breakthrough of the Story	20
	2.4 Continuance of the Story	22
	2.5 Prospects of the Story	23
Chapter 3	Practical Insights into Tourist Guide	32
	3.1 Career Definition	34
	3.2 Classification of Tourist Guides	36
	3.3 Roles of Tourist Guide	45

V

目 录

Chapter 4 Qualification and Training   56

     4.1 Qualification   60
     4.2 Certification   65
     4.3 Licensing   66
     4.4 Training   68

Chapter 5 Legal and Ethical Issues in Tour Guiding   80

     5.1 Legal Requirement   83
     5.2 Code of Practice   89
     5.3 Ethical Obligations   92

Chapter 6 Job Description of Guiding Group   102

     6.1 Tour Manager   105
     6.2 Tour Operator   106
     6.3 Tour Leader   108
     6.4 Tour Escort   110
     6.5 Local Tour Guide   111
     6.6 On-Site Guide   113

Chapter 7 Essential Steps for Guiding   122

     7.1 Pre-Tour Arrangement   125
     7.2 Meeting the Group   130
     7.3 Checking-in the Hotel   134
     7.4 Conducting the Tour   136

     7.5 Other Services 138
     7.6 Seeing the Group Off 140
     7.7 After Service Settlement 141

Chapter 8 Presentation Techniques 150

     8.1 Voice Projection, Diction, Microphone Use,
       Breathing Techniques 153
     8.2 Eye Contact and Body Language 157
     8.3 Style and Vocabulary 160
     8.4 Required Language Skills 162

Chapter 9 Communication Techniques 176

     9.1 Interpersonal Skills 179
     9.2 Stress Management 181
     9.3 Time Management 185

Chapter 10 Group Management 198

     10.1 Group Types 200
     10.2 Group Development 202
     10.3 Positioning of the Group 204
     10.4 Risk Management 205
     10.5 Conflict Management 206

Appendix 228

参考文献 238

Chapter 1

Introduction to the Course

Learning Outcome

After reading this chapter, you will be able to:

- Understand why you should learn this course
- Know what we are striving to do in this textbook
- Recognize whom this course is intended for
- Identify the course structure
- Be aware of the teaching and learning strategies
- Understand how you will be assessed
- Recognize the week-by-week course content

Opening Case

The president of the World Federation of Tourist Guide Associations (WFTGA), Ros Newlands, collected her Order of the British Empire (OBE) from a Snowy Buckingham Palace on Friday 17 December 2010. She was awarded the OBE for services to the tourism industry.

Ros has been a Scottish Blue Badge Tourist Guide since 1983. In addition to this and her global role in WFTGA, she is also a course director for the two-year Scottish Tourist Guide Training Course at the University of Edinburgh. In a recent press release, Ros states, "qualified tourist guides are ambassadors for their home countries and are often the only people that visitors really talk to and engage with. It is a great honor for a professional tourist guide to be recognized in this way."

(Source: Guidelines Internetion@l, Issue No. 15, December 2010.)

1. Why Ros Newlands was awarded her Order of the British Empire (OBE) from a Snowy Buckingham Palace?

2. Do you agree with the statement that qualified tourist guides are ambassadors for their home countries?

Introduction

The purpose of this introductory chapter is to provide an overview of the textbook's structure and contents before you really start this course. In doing so, it explains why we have this textbook, and how you should learn this course.

1.1 Textbook at a Glance

Why a textbook on *"Essentials for English-Speaking Tourist Guide: Theory and Practice"*? There are many reasons, and I would like to boil them down into two:

Early since 1979 when China opened its door to the outside world, millions of international tourists rush to China, and they do need professional tourist guide with excellent language and guiding skills. Nevertheless, the "Opinions of the State Council on Accelerating the Development of Tourism Industry" (State Council Order No. 41 [2009]) states that China will take efforts to make tourism industry a strategic backbone industry of the national economy and make it a more satisfactory modern service industry to the people. Without doubt, tourist guides in China play a vital role in realizing the goal of making tourism industry more satisfactory for tourists at home and abroad. As teachers in tourism and experienced tourist guides, we feel it our duty and honor to write this textbook to help those who are willing to be an excellent English-speaking tourist guide and who are on the way to do so. All the above may serve as macro-motives for the creation of this textbook.

The other, still more immediate purpose is to develop in students' knowledge and skills required in their future career as a tourist guide. During the past ten years or so, textbooks on knowledge and skills in tour guiding were mainly written in Chinese. To train the future tourist guide in English is definitely a great challenge for both students and teachers, and that primarily calls for a well-arranged textbook written in English with necessary references or information in Chinese to help them find the way to achieve the goal.

Introduction to the Course

Knowledge Links [1-1]

> 《国务院关于加快发展旅游业的意见》(国发[2009]41号,以下简称《意见》)于2009年12月1日正式发布。《意见》从贯彻落实科学发展观的高度,提出了加快发展旅游业的新任务、新要求、新内涵,对旅游业提出了全新的定位,指出了把旅游业培育成国民经济的战略性支柱产业和人民群众更加满意的现代服务业的宏伟目标,并就新时期旅游业发展进行了全面部署,明确了具体的发展目标。
>
> 《意见》被社会各界一致认为是一个具有里程碑意义的重要文件,是我国改革开放以来发展旅游业30年实践总结和全行业智慧的结晶,也是推动未来30年发展新格局的标志性新起点。

This textbook features a host of innovations and changes in both format and content, which makes it distinguished from a number of tourist guide-training textbooks on the bookshelf. Some were made as a result of feedback obtained from students, lecturers and professionals from tourism sector, in an effort to shape the textbook more user-friendly while maintaining the strengths for which it strives to achieve. Through all of these innovations and changes, however, a basic principle is to follow that "knowledge and skills are *dimensions* of each other, *interrelated* and *inseparable*". Hopefully, this textbook will assist such an effort. In this textbook, primarily we strive to:

- Present the *profession* of tour guiding as knowledge and skills paired.
- Emphasize problem-solving tools and practical skills rather than *pat* answers.
- Focus on knowledge, principles, idea, thought and experience essential for being a professional tourist guide.
- Attach great importance on learning through experiencing by providing a framework or essential know-how for students to get to know the whole from *sampling* a part of the real field experiences, observation and practice.

- Finally and most fundamentally, make it act as a guidebook to help students prepare for the certified tourist guide examination in China and see their successful professional career in the future.

1.2 Structure of Each Chapter

Several features have been developed for this textbook to understand the material more easily and to help bring the tour guiding profession alive.

- *Learning Outcome* lists specific learning objectives at the beginning of each chapter to help students focus their efforts and alert them to the important concepts, knowledge or skills.
- *Opening Case* introduces the main topics of the chapter by discussing a related case.
- *Introduction* briefly pictures the chapter.
- *Text* is the major reading material for students to learn.
- *Knowledge Links* are sources or references either in Chinese or in English by providing related information to assist your learning.
- *Summary* provides a concise *synopsis* of the topic presented.
- *Choice Questions* are for reviewing what you have learned in the text. You need to correctly answer 3 of the 5 questions to pass.
- *Review Questions* test students' recall and understanding of the key points learned.
- *Group Discussion* is the self-conducted activity to discuss the debating cases or phenomenon in guiding practice or tourism industry.
- *Guiding Exercise* is the assignment for students to practice guiding skills.
- *Translation Exercise* provides opportunity for students to practice English to Chinese translation skills, or vice versa.

- ***Case Study*** is designed to help students have in-depth understanding of the chosen topic by discussing a selected case.
- ***Further Reading*** provides supplementary reading materials for students to further explore.
- ***Key words and Phrases*** are ***highlighted***, and a list of them appears at the end of each text.

1.3 Level of the Textbook

This textbook is intended for junior or senior college students majoring in tourism management, or readers who are already tourist guides or who are aspiring to become a tourist guide whose English proficiency is above CET-4 or equivalent, while having good command of basic knowledge and skills required in travel and tourism industry.

1.4 Course Structure

This textbook contains ten chapters, which could be roughly divided into three parts.

Part one is an introduction to the course. Part two includes history of tourist guide, practical insight into tourist guide, and qualification and training for tourist guide, legal and ethical issues in tour guiding, and job description. Part three discusses guiding techniques ranging from essential guiding steps, presentation techniques, and communication techniques to group management.

1.5 Teaching and Learning Strategies

This course is delivered through a combination of formal lectures, in-class discussions, case studies and presentations. The course consists of 10 weekly sessions, each session comprising of a 90 minute lecture twice a week.

After the lecturers introduce knowledge and skills, the tutorial activities are aimed at demonstrating the application of knowledge and skills in tour guiding practices. Please note that students are required to individually complete exercises, engage in self-directed study, and actively participate in and contribute to class discussions. There is *considerable* reading required, so if satisfactory progress is to be made, every student needs to come to class prepared.

1.6 Assessment Details

The assessment will take the form of a single end-of-semester paper exam, plus oral test. The paper exam will be either 1 hour long or 90 minutes. The oral test lasts about 15 minutes. It is to test student's guiding skills, including *commentary*, interpretation and Q&A.

1.7 Teaching Plan

The course requires students to commit 52 learning hours (one learning hour equals to 45 minutes). Of this, there will be 50 hours of class support, and 2 hours of fieldwork. Students will have chances to visit travel agency and scenic spots during the field study.

Please note that times and contents are subject to change if and when required (Table 1.1).

Table1.1 Week-by-Week Course Content

Week	Course module	Hours
1	Chapter 1: Introduction to the Course	90/2
2	Chapter 2: Tour Guiding: Its Origin, Growth and Future	90/2
3	Chapter 3: Practical Insight into Tourist Guide	90/2
4	Chapter 4: Qualification and Training for Tourist Guide	90/2
5	Chapter 5: Legal and Ethical Issues in Tour Guiding	90/2
6	Chapter 6: Job Description of the Guiding Group	90/2
7	Chapter 7: Essentials Steps for Guiding	90/2
8	Chapter 8: Presentation Techniques	90/2
9	Chapter 9: Communication Techniques	90/2
10	Chapter 10: Group Management	90/2

Summary

Summary

This introductory chapter presents an overview of the textbook and the tour-guiding course as well. As discussed, there are two reasons for having this course: First, help those who want to be an excellent tourist guide; Second, facilitate future and present tourist guide with both knowledge and skills.

Following the basic principle of "knowledge and skills are dimensions of each other, interrelated and inseparable", this book designs 10 featured elements to assist students.

The textbook covers 10 chapters or 3 parts, and it is intended for junior or senior college students in tourism management, professional tourist guides, and readers who are determined to become one.

This course is delivered through a combination of formal lectures, in-class discussions, case studies and presentations, lasing about 10 weekly sessions and requiring students to commit 52 learning hours.

Key Words and Phrases

Dimension /dɪˈmenʃ(ə)n, daɪ-/ *noun*: a part of something.

Interrelated /ˌɪntəriˈleɪtɪd/ *adjective*: to have a close or shared relationship.

Inseparable /ɪnˈsep(ə)rəb(ə)l/ *adjective*: not able to be separated.

Profession /prəˈfeʃ(ə)n/ *noun*: a type of job that requires special education, training, or skill.

Pat /pæt/ *noun*: learned completely or perfectly.

Sampling /ˈsæmplɪŋ/ *noun*: a small group of people or things taken from a larger group and used to represent the larger group.

Synopsis /sɪˈnɒpsɪs/ *noun*: a short description of the most important information about something.

Highlight/ˈhaɪˌlaɪt/ *noun/verb*: to make or try to make people notice or be aware of (someone or something).

Considerable /kənˈsɪd(ə)rəb(ə)l/ *adjective*: large in size, amount, or quantity.

Commentary /ˈkɒmənt(ə)ri/ *noun*: spoken or written discussion in which people express opinions about someone or something; a spoken description of an event as it is happening.

Review Questions

1. Why a textbook on "Essentials for English-Speaking Tourist Guide: Theory and Practice"?
2. What do we strive to do in this textbook?
3. How many parts are included in each chapter?
4. Who should learn this textbook?
5. How is the textbook structured?
6. How many hours and weeks do you need to spend in learning this course?

Choice Questions

Choose the best answer to the questions below. You need to correctly answer 3 of the 5 questions to pass.

1. In this book, which feature is designed to assist your learning by providing sources or references either in Chinese or in English?

   A. Learning Outcome

   B. Knowledge Links

   C. Further Reading

   D. Case Study

2. Who is the person that this textbook is not intended for?

A. Junior or senior college students

B. Readers who are already tourist guides

C. Those who are aspiring to become a tourist guide

D. Whose English proficiency is below CET-4

3. How many chapters are included in this book?

A. 12

B. 9

C. 8

D. 10

4. How many learning hours do you need to spend in exploring this book?

A. 80

B. 48

C. 52

D. 120

5. Knowledge and skills are dimensions of each other, interrelated and inseparable.

A. True

B. False

Group Discussion

A guide can make or break a destination. In the current global economic climate, it is even more important that those who travel receive the best quality products and services. Some unqualified guides work mostly through commissions and tips and do not offer a professional service to visitors.

(Source from: Guidelines International, Issue No. 15, December 2010.)

1. Do you agree with the statement that "a guide can make or break a destination"?

2. Discuss why a "Tourist Guide Training Course" is so important in training qualified tourist guide.

Guiding Exercise

Mr. and Mrs. Smith are from the United Sates of America. They are taking flight CA1302 from *Los Angles* to *Beijing*. On behalf of China Youth Travel Agency, you are going to meet them at *Beijing* Capital International Airport.

You should prepare a board with basic information of the couple and sincerely wait outside the gate. After greeting the tourists, you are supposed to usher them to the car at the parking lot. Please remind them of having all their luggage or belongings taken, and make sure everyone board the car.

Translation Exercise

1. Please translate the following passage into Chinese.

The tourism industry is a strategic industry with low consumption of resources, good promoting co-efficient, plenty job opportunities and sound comprehensive benefits. Since the reform and opening to the outside world, Chinese tourism industry has been developing rapidly, the industrial scale has been expanding incessantly and the industrial system is becoming more and more perfect.

At present, China is at the rapid development stage towards industrialization and urbanization. The increasingly popular and diversified consumption demands provide new opportunities for the development of the tourism industry. In order to give full play to the tourism industry's positive roles in ensuring the growth, boosting the domestic demands and adjusting the structure, we hereby put forward the following opinions on accelerating the development of tourism industry.

2. Please translate the following passage into English.

《国务院关于加快发展旅游业的意见》指出，到2015年，旅游市场规模进一步扩大，国内旅游人数达33亿，年均增长10%；入境过夜游客人数达

9000万，年均增长8%；出境旅游人数达8300万，年均增长9%。旅游消费稳步增长，城乡居民年均出游超过2次，旅游消费相当于居民消费总量的10%。

经济社会效益更加明显，旅游业总收入年均增长达到12%以上，旅游业增加值占全国国内生产点值的比重提高到4.5%，占服务业增加值的比重达到12%。每年新增旅游就业人数达50万。

旅游服务质量明显提高，市场秩序明显好转，可持续发展能力明显增强，力争到2020年，我国旅游产业规模、质量、效益基本上达到世界旅游强国水平。

Case Study

2012年12月，成都某旅行社接待英国某旅游团。按照合同约定，该旅行团在成都游览7天，其中12月2日游览西岭雪山景区。甲旅行社委派导游李某担任该团陪同。李某无正当理由，而且也未征得该旅游团的同意，擅自对游览日程进行了变更，将游览西岭雪山行程取消，改为成都市内一日游。旅游团对此变更曾提出质疑，但导游员李某未进行解释。

该团离开成都之时，书面向成都市旅游局投诉，称导游李某未征得旅游者同意，擅自变更接待计划，违反了合同约定，使该旅游团未能游览西岭雪山景区，旅行社应承担赔偿责任。旅行社辩称，变更旅游行程属导游员个人行为，与旅行社无关；而导游员李某则辩称，造成未能游览西岭雪山的原因是西岭雪山景区大雪封山，接到了旅游局发布的不适宜旅游的通知，属于不可抗力，他本人可以不承担赔偿责任。

1. 导游员李某的辩称合理吗？如果不合理，其行为应受到什么样的处罚？
2. 旅行社的辩称合理吗？如果不合理，应受到什么样的处罚？

Further Reading

FACET Golden Guide Awards: Outstanding Tourist Guides

In 1998, the Forum Advocating Cultural & Eco Tourism Inc. (FACET) initiated and developed the FACET Golden Guide Award or Western Australian Tourism Awards. FACET is one of Western Australia's leading networking, professional development and information resources for people interested in cultural, nature based and eco-tourism and has a particular focus on how this type of tourism impacts on, and supports, community development and the environment.

The aim of the Award is to acknowledge individual excellence in tour guiding and raise the profile of this important profession.

This category recognizes the significant contribution that quality tourist guides make in providing memorable experiences to visitors through interpreting the natural and cultural environment in a responsible manner. It is designed to encourage individual tourist guides to create and deliver innovative, accurate, authentic and inspiring tours that will enhance tourism product and enrich the visitor experience.

This award is for an individual tourist guide demonstrating excellence in tour guiding. Eligibility includes tourist guides and coach captains working in the natural, cultural and heritage environments, in either a paid or volunteer capacity. Tourist guides who work on multiple tours should preferably focus on one tour, but can provide examples from other tours in addressing the following criteria.

(Source: http://www.tourismcouncilwa.com.au/wa-tourism-awards.)

Chapter 2

Tour Guiding: Its Origin, Growth and Future

Learning Outcome

After reading this chapter, you will be able to:

- Understand that the profession of tour guiding began as countries, civilizations and economies developed
- Know tourist guide's job description under the advent of Mass Tourism, Spas and Grand Tour in the 17th and 18th centuries
- See the great breakthrough of the story when the legend of Thomas Cook and his successors began in 19th century
- Identify modern tourism as a twentieth-century phenomenon
- Prospect the bright future of tour guiding career
- Learn how to deliver a Welcome Speech

Opening Case

The Leaders' Declaration from the annual meeting of the G20 world leaders, held in Los Cabos, Mexico, on 18~19 June, 2012, recognizes "the role of travel and tourism as a vehicle for job creation, economic growth and development", and commits to "work towards developing travel facilitation initiatives in support of job creation, quality work, poverty reduction and global growth".

This is the first time that Travel & Tourism has been included in the G20 Leaders' Declaration and is the culmination of long-term efforts by the industry, led by UNWTO and World Travel Tourism Council (WTTC), to encourage world leaders to see the potential of Travel & Tourism to create millions of new jobs and billions of dollars of GDP (Gross Domestic Product).

According to WTTC, the industry will directly contribute $2 trillion in GDP and 100 million jobs to global economy in 2012. When the wider economic impacts of the industry are taken into account, Travel & Tourism is forecasted to contribute some $6.5 trillion to the global economy and generate 260 million jobs —— or 1 in 12 of all jobs on the planet. G20 economies could boost their international tourist numbers by an additional 122 million, generate an extra $ 206 billion in tourism exports and create over five million additional jobs by 2015 (WTTC, 2012).

(Source: http://www.wttc.org/news-media/news-archive/2012/g20-recognises- travel-tourism-driver-economic-growth-first-time-/.)

1. What is the significance of the news that the G20 world leaders have for the first time recognized the importance of Travel & Tourism as a driver of jobs, growth and economic recovery?

2. According to WTTC, to what extent will Travel & Tourism contribute to the global economy?

Introduction

This chapter provides a historical perspective on the evolution of tourism as a business activity while also examining tour guiding as a profession through ages.

Tour Guiding: Its Origin, Growth and Future

2.1 Beginning of the Story

Travel has existed since the beginning of time when primitive man set out, often travelling great distances, in search of food and clothing necessary for his survival. Throughout the course of history, people have travelled for purposes of trade, religious *conviction*, economic gain, war and migration (William, 2005). As countries, civilizations and economies developed, travel and tourism grew for business and pleasure.

With the ***Babylonian*** invention of money and the development of trade in 4000 BC, travel and tourism were invented. Not only were the Babylonians the first to grasp the idea of money and use it in business transactions, but they founded the travel business. Beginning in 2700 BC, the Egyptians started building pyramids as elaborate burial tombs. So wonderful were these tombs that they attracted large numbers of visitors. Around 1500 BC, Queen ***Hatshepsut*** took a cruise from Egypt to Punt (on the east coast of Africa); the journey is recorded in the temples of ***Deir el-Bahri*** at ***Luxor***. Another Egyptian, ***Harkhuf***, was an envoy of the *pharaoh* to ***Sudan***. He brought home a *pygmy* trained in native dances as a present for his ruler —— the first recorded *souvenir*. Early Egyptians also purchased ***bargains*** or specialties abroad for their friends and relatives.

The same stories repeated in Ancient Greece, the Roman Empire, Persia and the Silk Road. In 776 BC, the Greek citizens honored the god ***Zeus*** by organizing an athletic competition that led to the Olympic Games. The ***Phoenicians*** carried paying passengers around the Mediterranean. In the Roman era, wealthy aristocrats and high government officials also travelled for pleasure. Seaside resorts located at **Pompeii** and **Herculaneum** afforded citizens the opportunity to escape to their vacation **villas** for escaping the summer heat of Rome. Travel, except during the **Dark Ages**, has continued to grow, and throughout recorded history has played a vital role in the development of civilizations.

Tourism is a story that, like time, has no beginning or end, so does the beginnings of tour guiding as a profession. Historically, tour guiding is one of the oldest human activities. The origins of tourist guides can be traced at least as far back as ancient Greece, but along with the beginning of modern mass tourism they have become an important factor of the travel industry ever since (Branislav, 2010).

The most likely *scenario* is that in ancient times, when emperor, scholar, businessman and pilgrim traveled, they needed help. Perhaps the owners of inns or shops, or young people who earned the occasional coin or food by helping them in need were the first group of tourist guide. Therefore, the profession of tourist guide began with the demand driven opportunity.

Some 1900 years ago, **Plutarch** living at this focus of ancient tourism, had to watch the *"periegetai" or* "leaders around" everyday, as they were called in Greek (Ziegler, et al., 1919). Those "periegetai" were to be met in every place, where tourists or pilgrims could be expected. They were so prevalent that it was not considered unreasonable to fear that one could not escape from them even in the underworld.

Their reputation was notoriously bad, but on the other hand they were indispensible: how else could a stranger find his way through an unknown city if he had no host there, or how else could he get informed on the various local objects of interest? Even **Herodotus** sometimes got his information from such guides (Schmitzer, et. al., 1999). His writing around 490 BC, noted the **gullibility** of travelers and their exploitation by many clearly less than professional guides. Later, the guide fulfilled the role of tutor to those on the Grand Tour in the 17th and 18th centuries, conducting their charges while pointing out objects of interest.

2.2 Development of the Story

Historians suggest that the advent of **mass tourism** began in England during the industrial revolution with the rise of the middle class and relatively inexpensive transportation (William, 2005), and the development of *spas* and Grand Tours in the 17th and 18th centuries.

Knowledge Links [2-1]

> The Grand Tour was the traditional trip of Europe undertaken by mainly upper-class European young men. The custom flourished from about 1660 AD until the advent of large-scale rail transportation in the 1840s, and was associated with a standard itinerary. It served as an educational rite of passage.

Tourist guide mostly worked alone or with a handful of others began as a basic traveler's aid: taking visitors new to the country or city and showing them the direction of places to stay and eat as well as guiding them to the places they needed to go, whether for business, worship, or education. Their pay might be negotiated on the spot; many tourist guides had to trust the visitor to offer something more than heartfelt thanks. Tourist guides realized that creating a regular business, with published services and fees, would not only gain them more visibility and respectability, but a chance at making a steady living. They also believed that the value of offering not just "meet and great" kinds of services, but of putting together a package that would offer travelers a way to visit the places that they wanted to go, without worrying about accommodation and transportation. The tourist guide would earn commission for bringing the guest to the hotel or inn in the first place.

2.3 Breakthrough of the Story

The story saw a breakthrough with the seaside resorts of the 19th century and the spread of international tourism through the agency of Thomas Cook and his successors.

Thomas Cook is one of the earliest recorded tourist guides. An idea to offer excursions came to the 32 years old Thomas Cook while waiting for the *stagecoach* on the London Road. With the opening of the extended *Midland Counties Railway*, he arranged to take a group of 570 *temperance* campaigners from Leicester Campbell Street station to a *rally* in *Loughborough*, 11 miles away. On 5 July 1841, Thomas Cook arranged for the rail company to charge one shilling per person that included rail tickets and food for this train journey. This was the first privately chartered excursion train to be advertised to the general public; Cook himself acknowledged that there had been previous, unadvertised, private excursion trains. During the following 3 summers he planned and conducted outings for temperance societies and Sunday-school children. In 1844, the Midland Counties Railway Company agreed to make a permanent arrangement with him provided he found the passengers. This success led him to start his own business running rail excursions for pleasure, taking a percentage of the railway tickets.

On 4 August 1845, he arranged accommodation for a party to travel from Leicester to Liverpool. In 1846, he took 350 people from Leicester on a tour of Scotland; however his lack of commercial ability led him to bankruptcy. He persisted and succeeded when he claimed that he arranged for over 165 000 people to attend the Great Exhibition in London. 4 years later, he planned his first excursion abroad, when he took a group from Leicester to **Calais** to coincide with the **Paris Exhibition**. The following year he started his "grand circular tours" of Europe. During the 1860s, he took parties to Switzerland, Italy, Egypt and United States. Cook established "inclusive independent travel", whereby the traveler went independently but his agency charged for travel, food and accommodation for a fixed period over any chosen route.

Knowledge Links [2-2]

> **The Great Exhibition in London**
>
> The Great Exhibition of the Works of Industry of all Nations or The Great Exhibition, sometimes referred to as the Crystal Palace Exhibition in reference to the temporary structure in which it was held, was an international exhibition that took place in Hyde Park, London, from 1 May to 15 October 1851. It was the first in a series of World's Fair exhibitions of culture and industry that were to become a popular 19th-century feature.

With his son, John Mason Cook, he formed a partnership and renamed the travel agency as Thomas Cook and Son. They acquired business premises on Fleet Street, London. By this time, Cook had stopped personal tours and became an agent for foreign or domestic travel. The office also contained a shop that sold essential travel accessories including guide books, luggage, telescopes and footwear. Thomas saw his venture as both religious and social service; his son provided the commercial expertise that allowed the company to expand. In accordance with his beliefs, he and his wife also ran a small temperance hotel above the office. Their business model was refined by the introduction of the *hotel coupon* in 1866. *Detachable* coupons in a *counterfoil* book were issued to the traveler. These were valid for either a restaurant meal or an overnight hotel stay on Cook's list.

In 1865, the agency organized tours of the United States, picking up passengers from several departure points. John Mason Cook led the excursion which included tours of several Civil War battlefields. A brief but bitter partnership was formed with an American businessman in 1871 called Cook, Son and Jenkins; however after an *acrimonious* split the agency reverted back to its original name. A round the world tour started in 1872, which for 200 *guineas*, included a steamship across the Atlantic, a stage coach across America, a paddle steamer to Japan, and an overland journey across China and India, lasting 222 days. In 1874, Thomas Cook introduced "*circular notes*", a product that later became better known by American Express's brand, "*traveler's*".

Thomas Cook retired in 1879, moved back to Leicestershire, and lived quietly until his death in 1898. The firm's growth was consolidated by John Mason Cook and his two sons.

2.4 Continuance of the Story

Tourism as we know it today is distinctly a 20th-century phenomenon. The story continued with the whole movement accelerated by the jet airplane and *charter flights* from the mid-20th century. Within this process, tourism was seen as dispersing geographical event outwards from its origins in Britain and Western Europe and spreading socially from the upper classes, down through the middle ranks and ultimately to the mass working classes (Towner, 1995).

The creation of the commercial airline industry following World War II and the subsequent development of jet aircraft in the 1950s signaled the rapid growth and expansion of international travel. This growth led to the development of a major new industry: tourism. In turn, international tourism became the concern of a number of state governments because it not only provided new employment opportunities, but also produced a means of earning foreign exchange (William, 2005).

Today, it is difficult to perceive the organized tourism without the service of guides, both tour managers/tour leaders and tourist guides (Branislav, 2010).

2.5 Prospects of the Story

Tour guiding career opportunities should grow much faster than the average rate for all occupations throughout 2006~2016. In many parts of the world, tourist guide employment is a favored and accessible employment aspiration for a range of young people graduating from school or college. It allows individuals the option of working in pleasant and stimulating environments and provides relatively secure tourism employment for those prepared to devote both time and energy to their work.

As an employment, it is more likely to attract the type of person who may be described as energetic and self-starting in outlook. It is also regarded by some commentators as being one of the most important positions within the tourism/hospitality industry concerning the provision of high quality service and therefore satisfied visitors (Dickman, 1994).

Summary

Summary

This chapter looks at the history of tour guiding: its origin, growth and future. Travel and tourism grew for business and pleasure though it is difficult to say when tourism actually began. It is believed that the profession of tourist guide began with the development and rising of ancient civilizations.

The advent of mass tourism as well as spas and Grand Tours in the 17th and 18th centuries created many opportunities for tourist guide. The story of tourist guide saw a breakthrough in 19th century when the legend of Thomas Cook and his successors began. The story continued with the whole movement accelerated by the jet airplane and charter flights from the mid-20th century. Although tourism and the story of tourist guide seem to have no beginning or end, the future of the two is expected to be bright and prosperous.

Key Words and Phrases

Conviction /kənˈvɪkʃ(ə)n/ *noun*: a strong belief or opinion.

Babylonian /ˌbæbɪˈləʊnɪən/ *adjective*: of Babylonia. Babylonia was an ancient cultural region in central-southern Mesopotamia (present-day Iraq), with Babylon as its capital.

Hatshepsut /hætˈʃəpsʊt/ *noun*: the fifth pharaoh of the 18th dynasty of Ancient Egypt (1508 BC—1458 BC).

Deir el-Bahari: Temple of Queen Hatshepsut (哈特谢普苏特神庙).

Tour Guiding: Its Origin, Growth and Future

Luxor: *noun*: a city in Upper (southern) Egypt (卢克索).

Harkhuf: a governor of Upper Egypt in the 23rd century BC.

Pharaoh /ˈfəːrəʊ/ *noun*: a ruler of ancient Egypt.

Sudan /suːˈdɑːn, suːˈdan/ *noun*: officially the Republic of Sudan is a country in North Africa.

Pygmy /ˈpɪgmi/ *noun*: a member of a group of very small people who live in Africa.

Souvenir /ˌsuːvəˈnɪə/ *noun*: something that is kept as a reminder of a place you have visited, an event you have been to, etc.

Bargain /ˈbɑːgin/ *noun*: something that is bought or sold for a price which is lower than the actual value.

Zeus /ˈzjuːs/ *noun*: the "Father of Gods and men" and the god of sky and thunder in Greek mythology.

Phoenicia /fəˈniːʃə/ *noun*: an ancient civilization in Canaan.

Pompei /pɑmˈpei/ *noun*: an ancient city destroyed and completely buried during a long catastrophic eruption of the volcano Mount Vesuvius in the year AD 79.

Herculaneum /ˌhəːkjʊˈleiniəm/ *noun*: an ancient Roman town destroyed by volcanic flows in 79 AD.

Villas /ˈvilə/ *noun*: a house that you can rent and live in when on vacation.

Dark Ages: the concept of a period of intellectual darkness that supposedly occurred in Europe.

Scenario /səˈnɑːrɪəʊ/ *noun*: a description of what could possibly happen.

Plutarch /ˈpluːtɑk/ *noun*: a Greek historian, biographer, and essayist, known primarily for his *Parallel Lives* (《希腊罗马名人传》) and Moralia (《道德论集》).

Herodotus /hiˈrɒdətəs/ *noun*: an ancient Greek historian and lived in the 5th century BC (484 BC—425 BC), reputed as the "Father of History".

Gullibility /ˌgʌliˈbiləti/ *noun*: easily fooled or cheated.

Mass Tourism: greater numbers of people could begin to enjoy the benefits of leisure time with the improvements in technology, allowing the transport of large numbers of people in a short space of time to places of leisure interest.

Spas /spɑː/ *noun*: a place where water that has many minerals in it comes up naturally from the ground and where people go to improve their health by swimming in, bathing in, or drinking the water.

Stagecoach /ˈsteɪdʒkəʊtʃ/ *noun*: a large carriage pulled by horses that was used in the past to carry passengers and mail along a regular route.

Midland Counties Railway: a railway company in the United Kingdom which existed between 1832 and 1844.

Temperance /ˈtemp(ə)r(ə)ns/ *noun*: the practice of drinking little or no alcohol.

Rally /ˈræli/ *noun*: a public meeting to support or oppose someone or something.

Loughborough /ˈlʌfb(ə)rə, luff-bərə/ *noun*: a town within the Charnwood borough of Leicestershire, England.

Calais /ˈkæleɪ/ *noun*: a town in northern France.

Paris Exhibition: French Industrial Exposition of 1844.

Hotel Coupon: in marketing, a coupon is a ticket or document that can be exchanged for a financial discount or rebate when purchasing a product.

Detachable /dɪˈtætʃəbəl/ *adjective*: to separate (something) from something larger.

Counterfoil /ˈkaʊntəfɔɪl/ *noun*: the part of a check, ticket, etc., that can be kept as a record when it is torn off.

Acrimonious /ˌækrɪˈməʊnɪəs/ *adjective*: angry and bitter.

Guinea /ˈgɪni/ *noun*: a coin that was minted in the Kingdom of Great Britain and the United Kingdom between 1663 and 1813.

Circular Notes: a document request by a bank to its foreign correspondents to pay a specified sum of money to a named person.

Traveler's Cheque: also known as traveler's check, is a preprinted, fixed-amount cheque designed to allow the person signing it to make an unconditional payment to someone else as a result of having paid the issuer for that privilege.

Charter Flight: the business of renting an entire aircraft (i.e., chartering) as opposed to individual aircraft seats.

Tour Guiding: Its Origin, Growth and Future

Review Questions

1. Why is it difficult to say when travel and tourism actually began?

2. What was tourist guide's job in the 17th and 18th centuries?

3. What is the story of Thomas Cook and his successors began in 19th century?

4. What is your view on modern tourism as a twentieth-century phenomenon?

5. How do you think of the future of tour guiding as a profession?

Choice Questions

Choose the best answer to the questions below. You need to correctly answer 3 of the 5 questions to pass.

1. Egyptians were not only the first to grasp the idea of money and use it in business transactions, but they founded the travel business.

   A. True

   B. False

2. Tourism is a story that, like time, has no beginning or end, so does the beginnings of tourist guide as a profession.

   A. True

   B. False

3. What is not the suggested reason for the advent of mass tourism in England?

   A. Industrial revolution

   B. Rise of the middle class

   C. Relatively inexpensive transportation

   D. Increased population

4. According to the text, when did the story of tourist guide see a breakthrough?

A. 18th century

B. 19th century

C. 20th century

D. 21th century

5. What is the signal of the rapid growth and expansion of international travel in the 1950s?

A. Hotel coupon

B. Paris Exhibition

C. The grand tour

D. The creation of the commercial airline industry

Group Discussion

Tourist guide is regarded as being one of the most important positions within the tourism/hospitality industry. In many parts of the world, tourist guide employment is a favored and accessible employment aspiration for a range of young people graduating from school or college.

1. Discuss why tourist guide is regarded as being one of the most important positions within the tourism/hospitality industry.

2. Discuss why tourist guide employment is a favored and accessible employment aspiration for a range of young people graduating from school or college.

Guiding Exercise

After meeting a group of tourists from United Kindom at Chengdu Shuangliu International Airport, you are taking a shuttle bus from the airport to the Chengdu Jinjiang Hotel.

Tour Guiding: Its Origin, Growth and Future

You are supposed to deliver a sincere and warm welcome speech which is suggested to include the following contents:
- Welcoming tourists and introducing the team.
- Describing the location.
- Introducing special events and offers.
- Offering advice.
- Closing remarks.

Translation Exercise

1. Please translate the following passage into Chinese.

Travel & Tourism continues to be one of the world's largest industries. Over the next 10 years, this industry is expected to grow by an average of 4% annually, taking it to 10% of global GDP, or some $10 trillion. By 2030, China will be the world's largest tourism destination.

2. Please translate the following passage into English

导游活动历史悠久，早在 2.5 万年前即成为了早期人类的重要活动。伴随着大众旅游的兴起，导游活动演变为现代旅游产业的的重要组成部分，以至于很难想象现代旅游缺少导游服务会是什么样子。

Case Study

2011 年国庆节期间，Smith 一家三口报名参加了畅游旅行社组织的双飞九寨沟 3 日游散客团。根据合同约定，一家人应于 10 月 2 日晚在成都双流国际机场乘飞机赴九寨沟"九黄机场"，并于 10 月 4 日下午 6:30 乘坐当日最后一班飞机返回成都。

由于导游小王缺乏经验，对进店购物时间把握不准，延误了乘坐返程的飞机。导游告知一行人只能先在机场附近的酒店住一晚上，将机票改签至第二天早上的第一班飞机返回成都。三人无奈之下，只得接受导游的建议，并支付了酒店住宿费用。返回后，遂将小王及旅行社投诉至当地旅游质监部门，要求退还酒店住宿费并提出了精神赔偿要求。

  1. 本案中旅行社是否承担责任？

  2. 导游员小王应该接受什么样的处罚？

  3. Smith一家提出的赔偿要求能否得到支持？

Further Reading

Welcome Speech

  Hello everyone. I am Jerry. On behalf of CITS, I'd like to extend a warm welcome to you all to Chengdu. This is our driver, Mr. Xu Fu. It is a great pleasure to meet you. We are just leaving the airport for your hotel. It will take us about 45 minutes to get there by bus.

  Please sit back and relax. I believe that you are going to enjoy your stay here in Chengdu. The city is strategically situated in the western part of Sichuan Province, extending about 166 kilometers from east to west, and 192 kilometers from north to south. This city is proud of its great cultural heritage and scenic beauties. The splendid past is shown by detailed historical descriptions, abounding historical sites and remains.

  During your stay here in Chengdu, we will visit the Royal Tomb of Wangjian, *Wuhou Temple*, Dufu's Thatched Cottage, River Viewing Pavilion Park and Qingyang Temple. Nevertheless, the city is not only known for her history of more than 2 300 years, but also noted for her leisurely lifestyle. You may like to go to a tea house, relax in a bamboo chair, order a cup of tea or buy a newspaper and flip through the pages. You may doze off in all the comfort or sip tea while watching performances, such as tea art, fire breathing or acrobatics. The leisurely pace and idleness of Chengdu is also reflected in its varied local snacks. They are delicious yet inexpensive, and a food break is a good way to kill time. After dusk on a summer's day, the locals like to go out and sit on the dykes of the Jinjiang River to drink beer, eat snacks, and enjoy the surroundings.

  If you need to exchange your dollars into RMB, please use a bank or money exchange. We don't recommend exchanging your money at the hotel because you won't get a fair rate. Also, if you want to get around the city, we recommend that you take a taxi. If you have any further question, please do not hesitate and feel free to let me know. We feel much honored to serve you.

Ladies and Gentlemen, we're going to arrive at the hotel in just a few minutes. Please sit back and enjoy the view of the city. Please double check to make sure that your bag is taken off the bus.

Wish you have a pleasant stay here and a wonderful vacation in Chengdu.

Chapter 3
Practical Insights into Tourist Guide

Learning Outcome

After reading this chapter, you will be able to:

- Discuss different career definitions of tourist guide
- Identify different terms used to describe the career of tourist guide
- Know the classification of tourist guide
- Realize the progression of the roles of tourist guide in history

Opening Case

In the United Kingdom and Mainland China, acceptance of commissions and/or tips are frowned upon or forbidden. By contrast, In Hong Kong SAR, commissions form the largest part of a guide's income (44%).

The practice of not accepting commission has merits and undoubtedly raises the professionalism of guiding in countries that adopt such practices. However, one needs to recognize that majority of tourist Guides in China do not enjoy the benefits of a minimum wage. Hence, one might not necessarily frown upon the practice of accepting commissions.

(Source: Ap J, Wong K K F. Case study on tour guiding: professionalism, issues and problems. Tourism Management. 2001, 22(5), 551-563.)

1. Please tell the advantages and disadvantages of the commission practice in the United Kingdom, Mainland China, and Hong Kong SAR.

2. Please discuss the practice of not accepting commission in China.

Introduction

This chapter takes a practical insight into the profession of tourist guide. To begin with, it discusses career definitions of tourist guide, and then it further clarifies various kinds of tourist guides based on different perspectives. Lastly it talks about roles that guides play.

Chapter 3

3.1 Career Definition

A number of terms are in use to describe those whose responsibility is to **shepherd** and inform groups of tourists. Initially being a term primarily used in the US market, tourist guide is perhaps the most commonly applied to describe the role, although there are other terms used include tour leader, tour captain, tour escort, tour manager, tourist guide, and *courier*.

While the definitions of tourist Guide varied, an internationally accepted definition given by **the International Association of Tour Managers (IATM)**, **the European Federation of Tourist Guide Associations (EFTEG)** and European Normalization Body (ENB) which was finally approved in 1998 is that "a tourist guide is a person who guides groups or individual visitors from abroad or from the home country around the monuments, sites and museums of a city or region; to interpret in an inspiring and entertaining manner, in the language of the visitor's choice, the cultural and natural heritage and environment" (EFTEGA,1998).

Knowledge Links [3-1]

> 国家旅游局于1999年10月1日颁布的《导游人员管理条例》规定：导游人员是指依照本条例的规定取得导游证，接受旅行社委派，为旅游者提供向导、讲解及相关旅游服务的人员。

Another definition provided by the Professional Tourist Guide Association of San Antonio (PTGASA) is that the guide is "a person with an effective combination of enthusiasm, knowledge, personality qualities and high standards of conduct and ethics who leads groups to the important sites, while providing interpretation and commentary" (PTGASA, 1997). This definition differs slightly from *the European Committee for Standardization (CEN)* one in that it focuses upon the importance of the personality and conduct of the guide as essential ingredients that constitute the work of the tourist guide (John Ap, Kevin K.F. Wong, 2000).

CEN defines tourist guide as "a person who guides visitors in the language of their choice and interprets the cultural and natural heritage of an area, which person normally possesses an area-specific qualification usually issued and/or recognized by the appropriate authority" [EN 13809: 2003].

New European standard EN 15565, 2008 on Training and Qualification of Tourist Guides in Europe states that Tourist Guides are representatives of cities, regions and countries for which they are qualified. It depends largely on them if visitors feel welcome, want to stay longer or decide to come back. They therefore contribute considerably to the perception of the destination. Tourist Guides are able to help travelers understand the culture of the region visited and the way of life of its inhabitants. They have a particular role on the one hand to promote the cultural and natural heritage whilst on the other hand to help ensure its sustainability by making visitors aware of its importance and vulnerability.

Tourist Guide (or tour guide) provides assistance, information and cultural, historical and contemporary heritage interpretation to people on organized tours, individual clients, educational establishments, at religious and historical sites, museums, and at venues of other significant interest. They, normally, have a recognized national or regional tourist guide qualification.

Tourist Guide has also been described as "an information giver and *fount* of knowledge", "*mentor*" (Cohen, 1985), "*mediator*" (de Kadt, 1979; Nettekoven, 1979), and "*culture broker*" (McKean, 1976). The mediator and cultural broker functions, as suggested here, refers to the interpretive aspects of the tourist guide's work which plays a vital role in enhancing the visitors' experience at a destination and their understanding of the destination and its culture (John Ap, Kevin K.F. Wong, 2000).

3.2 Classification of Tourist Guides

3.2.1 Based on Time of Working

- **Full-time tourist guide/Professional tourist guide**

Full-time tourist guides take guiding career as a full time job, and are more likely to be highly educated and formally trained and possess a license to practice professionally.

In other words, they are full-time licensed guides registered in the agent of official tourism boards and are under legal obligation to the employer or travel agency (or company).

- **Part-time tourist guide/ Freelance guide**

Part-time tourist guides or freelance guides take guiding career as a temporary or part-time job, attracting teachers, actors and others with a good knowledge of foreign languages. Their services are usually offered on a freelance basis.

They usually work on a contract basis per tour and provide visitors to an area with local tour *narration* and navigation. They are frequently hired by tour managers or tour operators who are traveling to your city from overseas. Some of them are also private tour specialists and offer their services to any group of tourists no matter how small to lead them around the city, offer translation services and give them tips and advices for the tour. Private guides will normally meet the travelers at the airport and lead them to various locations and attractions each day. Freelance guides can charge on a per tour basis if working with an accredited operator or director, but may decide to charge per hour or per day if leading private tours, depending on the requirements of the visitors.

- **Volunteer Guides**

One of the best ways to gain experience in the tour guiding industry and to enjoy traveling at the same time is to volunteer for various tours. Museum guides in China are often hired on a voluntary basis.

3.2.2 Based on Working Duties

- **Tour Manager/Tour Director**

Tour Manager is a person who manages and supervises the itinerary on behalf of the tour operator, ensuring the program is carried out as described in the tour operator's literature and sold to the traveler/consumer and who gives local practical information.

Tour managers may or may not be tourist guides as well. They are not trained or licensed to work in specific areas unless they have the proper requirements or legal right, depending on the region.

Knowledge Links [3-2]

> 组团旅行社（以下简称组团社）是从事招徕、组织旅游者，并为国内旅游、入境旅游、出境旅游的旅游者提供全程导游服务的旅行社。
> 接待旅行社（以下简称接待社）是受组团社委托，实施组团社的接待计划，委派地方陪同导游员，安排旅游团（者）在当地参观游览等活动的旅行社。

- **Tour Leaders**

Tour leader is someone who leads a group overseas. They may or may not have visited the place prior. Their job *entails* ensuring the people get what they paid for, facilitating the flight, and making sure the people have a good time.

They take a person to see a doctor or throw a "welcome cocktail party" on arrival. They work together with the tourist guide and sometimes a national guide as well. They may be paid by the Tour Operator who planned the trip or sometimes a travel agent who put the trip together. A professional tour leader typically will lead about a dozen trips a year.

Knowledge Links [3-3]

> 出境旅游领队人员（以下简称领队），是指依照《出境旅游领队人员管理办法》规定取得出境旅游领队证（简称"领队证"），接受具有出境旅游业务经营权的国际旅行社（以下简称"组团社"）的委派，从事出境旅游领队业务的人员。

- **Tour Escort**

Tour escort in China is also known as national guide, who is the representative of a tour operator provides basic assistance to travelers and leads a group throughout a country or part of a country.

Their job entails providing commentary, routing the tour, timing the tour and looking after *logistics* like hotel check-ins and reservations for attractions. They are paid by the tour operator and typically work fulltime for the tour season. In general, a tour escort differs slightly and is characterized by the fact that they travel on longer tours, often overnight.

Knowledge Links [3-4]

> 全程陪同（以下简称全陪），是受组团社委派，作为其代表，监督接待社和地方陪同导游员的服务，以使组团社的接待计划得以按约实施，并为旅游团（者）提供全旅程陪同服务的导游员。

- **Local Guides**

For pleasure and discovery, a traveler can take a tour of the city by motor

Practical Insights into Tourist Guide 39

coach, van, taxi or bus, or as part of a walking tour.

The person who points out and comments on the highlights of the city is called a city guide or local guide. When the local guide doubles the duty by driving the vehicle, that person becomes the driver-guide.

Knowledge Links [3-5]

> 地方陪同导游员（以下简称地陪），是受接待社委派，代表接待社实施旅游行程接待计划，为旅游团（者）提供当地导游服务的导游员。

- **On-site Guides**

If you went to the Mt. E'mei, the person who took you on tour of the sight is called an on-site guide. This guide conducts the tour of a specific building or a limited area. These tours can be taken by walking.

Another type of on-site guide working free of charge or voluntarily may be called a *docent*. A docent specifically works at a museum.

- **Specialized Guides**

This category of guide has particular skills that are unique to match the client's needs. These guides may conduct bike tours, white water rafting trips, hiking expeditions or on tours that are more physically demanding and unusual. This will be backpack hiking in the Grand Canyon National Park, Arizona, USA or in Jiuzhaigou Valley, West Sichuan.

3.2.3 Based on Working Place

As long as tourist guide is the *generic* term used to classify all forms of travel group leaders including those working on motor coaches, trains, on cruise ships, or on walking tours, the following are several of them:

- **Sightseeing Tourist Guide**

A sightseeing tourist guide will work *predominantly* on tour buses or motor coaches.

Sightseeing tourist guides will often need to drive the tour bus, as well as provide the narration for the tour. Sightseeing tourist guides are usually employed by a tour director. They are chosen for specific tours depending on their skills and knowledge of an area.

- **Step-on Tourist Guide**

A step-on tourist guide is hired by a tour director or tourist guide to provide specific information regarding a particular sight or attraction.

As the name suggests, they step onto the bus or train for a certain portion of the tour. The tourist guide in charge will make use of a step-on tourist guide when entering a large national park or attraction like Disney World. In this instance, the step-on guide has far more intricate knowledge about the location. Step-on tourist guides are based in the area where they lead tours and usually work for a private company, museum, national park, or resort.

- **Shore Excursion Guide**

A shore excursion guide usually works on board a cruise *liner*, but can also work for a charter touring yacht, or river cruise vessel.

The shore excursion guides, also known as cruise hosts, will take groups of people from the cruise ship onto the shore at various ports along the journey and show them the main attractions. This requires a bit more research on the guide's behalf, as you will be required to learn about every port city you travel to along the way, and there can be quite a few on one cruise. The guides must be able to speak the local language and will need to know where to find the best shopping spots, ideal dining experience, organize tickets for museums and other attractions, as well as plan activities for the guests, such as water skiing, hiking, seeing a live theater or music performance and more. Shore excursion guides travel on the cruise ship as well, making this an exciting job to have, as you will get time off while at sea to explore the ship and take advantage of all the magnificent events and activities on board.

- **Adventure, Sport and Eco Tourist Guides**

Adventure and ecotourism is on the rise and with it comes the need for highly skilled adventure and eco tourist guides, as well as sports tourist guides.

They must be qualified and skilled in a certain type of sport and need to have a passion for adventure. Whether it is hiking through the Amazon, cycling through the French countryside, or leading a safari tour through the African *savannah*, adventure tourist guides must be responsible at all times. They have the lives of their tour group in their hands, and must be fully trained in emergency and first aid. On eco tours and adventure tours, mapping out routes and strategically planning each day is imperative, and you have to understand the climate, weather conditions, and geography and wildlife of the area in order to lead a safe and successful tour. Ecotourism guides aim to educate people about the natural environment they are traveling in. They encourage conservation and preservation of natural ecosystems as well as biodiversity.

3.2.4 Based on Working Language

- **Chinese Speaking Guides**

Mandarin, Tibetan, Dialects (Cantonese, Shanghai Dialect), etc.

- **Foreign Languages Speaking Guides**

English, German, French, Russian, Italian, Spanish, Japanese, Korean, etc.

3.2.5 Based on Level of Skills

1. Elementary Level

- Understand and abide by the general laws and tourism related ordinances of P.R. China.
- Represent the area (site, city, region and/or country), and be familiar with major tourist attractions in China.
- Grasp the knowledge of politics, economy, and history, geography, and culture of China.

- Understand and respect the cultural and folklore of the tourist market.
- Adhere to professional ethics and code of conduct.
- For those foreign language speaking tourist guides, their language proficiency shall be as good as those year 3 college students in the major of the chosen language other than Chinese; for those Chinese speaking ones, they shall have a good command of both written and speaking Chinese language equivalent to senior high school level.
- Be capable of fulfilling the guiding task independently, and have a good understanding of teamwork.
- Express him/herself fluently, accurately and coherently, and have elegant body language.
- Know how to fill in the forms related to guiding service, and write working report and memo.
- Provide the highest standard of service in an honest and fair manner, and him/herself service is satisfied by 85 percent of tourists.
- Foreign language speaking tourist guides shall have an advanced diploma of the chosen language other than Chinese, a bachelor's degree or above; Chinese-speaking guides shall have a certificate equivalent to or above senior high school.

2. Intermediate Level

- Understand and abide by the general laws and tourism related ordinances of P.R. China.
- Represent the area (site, city, region and/or country), and be familiar with major tourist attractions in China.
- Grasp the knowledge of politics, economy, and history, geography, and culture of China.
- Understand and respect the cultural and folklore of the tourist market.
- Adhere to professional ethics and code of conduct.
- For those foreign language speaking tourist guides, their language proficiency shall be as good as those year 4 college students in the major of the chosen language other than Chinese; for those Chinese speaking ones, they shall have a good command of both written and speaking Chinese language equivalent to advanced diploma level.
- Have good guiding and communication skills, and be able to solve problems independently.

- Express him/herself fluently, accurately, and coherently, and understand a dialect in Chinese.
- Know how to train tourist guide at elementary level.
- Provide the highest standard of service in an honest and fair manner, and him/herself service is satisfied by 90 percent of tourists.
- Foreign language speaking tourist guides shall have an advanced diploma of the chosen language other than Chinese, a bachelor's degree or above; Chinese-speaking guides shall have a certificate equivalent to or above senior high school.
- Be eligible to apply for the intermediate level after receiving elementary one for at least two years.

3. Advanced Level

- Understand and abide by the general laws and tourism related ordinances of P.R. China.
- Represent the area (site, city, region and/or country), and be familiar with major tourist attractions in China.
- Have a wide range of knowledge.
- Understand and respect the cultural and folklore of the tourist market.
- Adhere to professional ethics and code of conduct.
- Foreign language speaking tourist guides shall have an advanced diploma of the chosen language other than Chinese, a bachelor's degree or above; Chinese-speaking guides shall have a certificate equivalent to or above senior high school.
- Have excellent guiding and communication skills; and be able to solve difficult problems independently.
- Be able to conduct research into tourism, and write commentaries.
- Express him/herself fluently, accurately, and coherently. Foreign language speaking tourist guides shall be able to do interpretation; Chinese tourist guides shall be fluent in both Chinese mandarin and a dialect.
- Know how to train tourist guide at intermediate level.
- Have a good professional reputation in China; provide the highest standard of service in an honest and fair manner, and him/herself service is satisfied by 95 percent of tourists.
- Foreign language speaking tourist guides shall have an advanced diploma of the chosen language other than Chinese, a bachelor's degree or

above; Chinese-speaking guides shall have a certificate equivalent to or above senior high school.
- Have recognized paper or report.
- Be eligible to apply for the intermediate level after receiving intermediate one for at least four years.

4. Expert Level

- Understand and abide by the general laws and tourism related ordinances of P.R. China.
- Represent the area (site, city, region and/or country), and be very familiar with major tourist attractions in China.
- Have a wide range of knowledge, and be expertise in some field associated with tourism.
- Understand and respect the cultural and folklore of the tourist market.
- Adhere to professional ethics and code of conduct.
- Foreign language speaking tourist guides shall be able to fluent in one chosen language other than Chinese, and be fairly fluent in a second foreign language; Chinese speaking ones shall have a good command of both written and speaking Chinese language, and be fairly fluent in a Chinese dialect.
- Have excellent guiding and communication skills with unique personality; and be able to solve difficult problems independently.
- Be able to conduct research into tourism, and write excellent commentaries.
- Express him/herself fluently, accurately, and coherently. Foreign language speaking tourist guides shall be able to do interpretation for formal meeting; Chinese tourist guides shall be fluent in Chinese mandarin and be capable of delivery commentary focusing on museum and architecture.
- Know how to train tourist guide at advanced level.
- Have a good professional reputation in China; provide the highest standard of service in an honest and fair manner, and him/herself service is satisfied by 98 percent of tourists.
- Foreign language speaking tourist guides shall have an advanced diploma of the chosen language other than Chinese, a bachelor's degree or above; Chinese-speaking guides shall have a certificate equivalent to or above senior high school.
- Have recognized paper or report published in some key academic journal.

- Be eligible to apply for the intermediate level after receiving advanced one for at least five years.

3.3 Roles of Tourist Guide

The role of a guide suffers from being largely a seasonal occupation (apart from those key year-round tourism centers such as London), and from offering little career progression. Thus, increasingly, the role is linked to that of entertainer or "*animator*" at heritage sites, with guides offering historical interpretation of the site while acting out roles in appropriate period costume. The role attracts those with both acting skills and local knowledge.

Knowledge Links [3-6]

> 导游的基本职责包括：①接受旅行社指派的接团任务，按接待计划，安排和组织旅游者参观游览；②负责向旅游者导游、讲解、传播中国文化；③配合和督促有关部门安排旅游者的吃、位、行、游、购、娱，保护旅游者的人身安全和财产安全等事项；④反映旅游者的意见和要求，协助安悻会见、座谈等活动；⑤解答旅游者的询问，协助处理旅途中遇到的问题。

Although the Oxford dictionary (Ludowyk and Moore, 1996) defines a guide simply as...a person who shows others the way, research has found the role of a tourist Guide is much broader (Cohen, 1985; Holloway, 1981). In a review about the origin, structure and dynamics of tour guiding, Cohen (1985) created a model based on its historic beginnings with the pathfinders and mentors of ancient times. He re-named these two roles to make them more relevant to modern tour guiding and called the pathfinder role "leadership", and the mentor role "mediatory". As a leader, the tourist Guide has to organize (i.e. provide direction, access, and control) and build the team (i.e. ensure group cohesion and morale). As a mentor, the guide acts as a "middleman" and is an educator for the group.

Cross (1991), Mancini (1990) and Pond (1993) provide useful practical hands-on information about tour guiding practice, professionalism, and address issues such as the role of guiding, guiding skills and techniques, and the problems and issues that a guide may face when leading a tour. Pond (1993), for example, indicated that a guide could play a role as:

- A leader capable of assuming responsibility;
- An educator to help the guest understand the places they visit;
- An ambassador who extends hospitality and presents the destination in a way that make visitors want to return;
- A host who can create a comfortable environment for the guest; and
- A facilitator who knows how and when to fulfill the previous four roles.

Summary

Summary

This chapter has taken a very practical insight into the profession of tourist guide.

Firstly, it is very important for readers to understand a list of terms describing those whose job is to shepherd and inform groups of tourists, amony which "tourist guide" is perhaps the most commonly used one. Since there are various career definitions of tourist guide, it is impossible to have an internationally accepted one. Probably only through discussion and comparison will we be able to appreciate what tourist guide looks like in the real world; and ultimately to get close to the true sense of it. After that, it goes to discuss classification of tourist guide. It is said that there are different kinds of tourist guide if you look at them from different perspectives. Finally, it explains the role that tourist guide plays.

Key Words and Phrases

Shepherd /ˈʃepəd/ *noun*: to guide (someone or something).

Courier /ˈkʊriə/ *noun*: a person whose job is to carry messages, packages, etc., from one person or place to another.

IATM: in 1962, 12 European Tour Managers met together in London to found the International Association of Tour Managers. Their purpose: to exchange information, views, experiences and difficulties encountered. At this stage, the Association was little more than a social club. Today, IATM has become to be recognized as a forum for professional tour managers, promoting their services and representing their views at national, European Union (EU) and international levels. Now truly an "International Association", IATM's members are to be found in EU member states, Switzerland, Norway, North America, Australasia, Israel and the Republic of China.

WFTGA: it came into being as a result of proposals put forward at the first International Convention of Tourist Guides, set up through the initiative of the Israel Guides' Association in February 1985. The Federation was officially registered as a non-profit organization under Austrian law after a second Convention held in Vienna in 1987, representing well over 88 000 individual tourist guides.

CEN: it is a non-profit organization whose mission is to foster the European economy in global trading, the welfare of European citizens and the environment by providing an efficient infrastructure to interested parties for the development, maintenance and distribution of coherent sets of standards and specifications.

Fount /ˈfaʊnt/ *noun*: the source of something. a fount of knowledge/ justice/ wisdom

Mentor /ˈmenˌtɔː/ *noun*: someone who teaches or gives help and advice to a less experienced and often younger person.

Mediator /ˈmiːdiˌeitə/ *verb*: a neutral party who assists in negotiations and conflict resolution, the process being known as mediation.

Culture Broker: a person who helps other people to reach agreements, to make deals, or to buy and sell property (such as stocks or houses).

Narration /nəˈreiʃ(ə)n/ *noun*: the act or process of telling a story or describing what happens.

Entail /inˈteil/ *verb*: to have (something) as a part, step, or result.

Logistics /ləˈdʒistiks/ *noun*: the things that must be done to plan and organize a complicated activity or event that involves many people.

Docent /ˈdəʊs(ə)nt/ *noun*: a person who leads guided tours especially through a museum or art gallery.

Generic /dʒiˈnerik/ *adjective*: of or relating to a whole group or class.

Predominant /priˈdɑːmənənt/ *adjective*: more important, powerful, successful, or noticeable than other people or things.

Liner /ˈlaɪnə/ *noun*: a large ship used for carrying passengers.

Savanna /səˈvænə/ *noun*: a savanna, or savannah, is a grassland ecosystem characterized by the trees being sufficiently small or widely spaced so that the canopy does not close.

Animator /ˈænɪˌmeɪtə/ *noun*: person who creates animated movies and cartoons.

Review Questions

1. What is your understanding of tourist guide?
2. How many kinds of tourist guide are there in the world?
3. What kind of tourist guide do you want to be?
4. What is the major role that a tourist guide should play?

Choice Questions

Choose the best answer to the questions below. You need to correctly answer 3 of the 5 questions to pass.

1. Which organ has defined tourist guide as "a person who guides visitors in the language of their choice and interprets the cultural and natural heritage of an area, which person normally possesses an area-specific qualification usually issued and/or recognized by the appropriate authority"?

   A. European Normalization Body

   B. The International Association of Tour Managers

C. The European Committee for Standardization

D. The Professional Tourist Guide Association of San Antonio

2. Who is the person leading a group overseas?

A. On-site Guides

B. Tour Escort

C. Tour Leaders

D. Local Guides

3. If you usually work on board a cruise liner, what kind of tourist guide you are most probably?

A. Step-on Tourist Guide

B. Shore Excursion Guide

C. On-site Guides

D. Specialized Guides

4. How many groups of tourist guides have been classified, based on level of skills?

A. 4

B. 5

C. 6

D. 3

5. Which is not the role that tourist guide should play, according to Pond (1993)?

A. A leader capable of assuming responsibility

B. An educator to help the guest understand the places they visit

C. An ambassador who extends hospitality and presents the destination in a way that makes visitors want to return

D. An entertainer who can create a comfortable environment for the guest

Group Discussion

There appears to be pressure put on the EU and possibly the CEN to renegotiate the definitions for tourist guide and possibly other tourism definitions. This pressure will be resisted by European Federation of Tourist Guide Association (FEG) and by many others involved in the extremely time-consuming process leading up to their agreement. This definition is also used as a normative reference (an accepted definition of what a tourist guide is) in EN 15565(WFTGA, 2010).

1. What is your interpretation of the EN 15565?

2. Why there is pressure put on the EU and possibly CEN to renegotiate the definitions for tourist guide?

Guiding Exercise

Ms. Wang, a local tour guide, was supposed to get to the Chengdu Shuangliu International Airport at 2:30 pm to meet her group from UK. Unfortunately, traffic block changed her plan. When she managed to arrive at the airport, it was close to 3:30 pm, and the guests had been there anxiously waitingand complaining.

1. What should Ms. Wang do in order to comfort the complained guests?

2. How to avoid this kind of embarrassed problems happen again?

Translation Exercise

1. Please translate the following passages into Chinese.

Tourist guides are representatives of the cities, regions and countries for which they are qualified. It depends largely on them if visitors feel welcome, want to stay longer or decide to come back. They therefore contribute considerably to the perception of the destination.

Tourist guides are able to help travelers understand the culture of the region visited and the way of life of its inhabitants. They have a particular role on the one hand to promote the cultural and natural heritage whilst on the other hand to help ensure its sustainability by making visitors aware of its importance and vulnerability.

2. Please translate the following passage into English.

导游人员是指依照《导游人员管理条例》的规定取得导游证，接受旅行社委派，为旅游者提供向导、讲解及相关旅游服务的人员。在中华人民共和国境内从事导游活动，必须取得导游证。

Case Study

张成与朋友一行三人报名参加了康达旅行社组织的九寨沟—黄龙 5 日游自由人团。根据合同约定，王征等人 6 月 2 日晚乘汽车赴九寨沟，6 月 6 日下午返程。结果就在 6 月 5 日，地接社导游告知张成，他们的旅游行程已结束，当天中午乘车返回。张成等 3 人无奈之下，只得提前返回。返回后，遂将旅行社投诉至当地旅游质监所，要求退还一天的导游服务费及相关费用。

旅行社辩称游客张成等人是临出发前一天才到旅行社报的名，九寨沟—黄龙 5 日游的对外报价是 3 080 元/人，张成等人当时要求不去黄龙，即给每人优惠 1 000 元，并说要马上签订合同，旅行社计调李默私自将原行程上的"黄龙"去掉后，以原行程为模本与王签订了合同。之后，地接社将九寨沟 4 日游的行程表发了过来，旅行社这才发现签订的合同行程多了一天，这次事故纯属导游李默的个人行为，旅行社不承担责任。

1. 你认为本案中旅行社是否承担责任？为什么？
2. 你认为应该如何避免类似纠纷的发生？

Further Reading

A BRIEF HISTORY OF WFTGA

WFTGA came into being as a result of proposals put forward at the first International Convention of Tourist Guides, in February 1985. The Federation was officially registered as a non-profit organization under Austrian law after a second convention held in Vienna in 1987. At each international convention the WFTGA grew and today the organization has members from more than 70 countries, representing well over 200 000 individual tourist guides, WFTGA has established an international network of professional tourist guides and today is the only global forum for tourist guides and continues to grow with the changes of this industry.

WFTGA is a not-for-profit, non-political organization. Its main purpose is to promote, market and ensure that tourist guides are recognized as the ambassadors of a region. They are the first and sometimes the only representation of the population a visitor will meet. WFTGA offers services to its members but also communicates to those in search of the services of professional area specific tourist guides and where to hire them. We also actively promote our members' associations and industry partners worldwide.

WFTGA encourages and supports the use of only area-specific tourist guides to member regions which keeps the local tourist guides working and ensures that visitors have accurate and professional services from our members' regions.

The day-to-day running of the World Federation is the responsibility of the Executive Board whose members are elected by delegates of the member countries for a two- year period at each convention. To take a position on the Executive Board one has to know that such a position means complete involvement, dedication and many hours of work. Executive Board members who are elected must be actively practicing tourist guides who are not tour operators, or tourist guide employers.

In addition, a number of Area Representatives are appointed by the Executive Board to provide liaison with the Board and with the existing members, and to encourage new membership. Both Executive Board Members and Area Representatives are active professional tourist guides. They are volunteers who dedicate their time and effort to achieving the aims of the Federation and to the promotion of tourist guides worldwide.

The official language of the World Federation of Tourist Guide Associations is English. However, the WFTGA 2005—2007 Executive Board represents the following languages: English, French, Arabic, Spanish, Italian, German, Russian, Greek, Armenian, Chinese and Turkish. We will be more than happy to assist anyone who has difficulty in communicating in English. The WFTGA logo is a symbol of the hands of friendship and guidance stretched across the world.

WFTGA is dedicated and committed:

- To establishing contact with tourist guide associations, individuals, tourism training institutes throughout the world and to reinforcing their professional ties
- To representing professional tourist guides internationally and to promoting and protecting their interests
- To enhancing the image of the profession and promoting the use of area specific local tourist guides in all regions
- To promoting a universal code of ethics and skills
- To raising, encouraging and establishing the highest standards of professionalism

- To developing international training, and improving the quality of guiding through education and training
- To facilitating the exchange of information between members.

(Source: http://www.wftga.org/.)

Chapter 4

Qualification and Training

Learning Outcomes

After reading this chapter, you will be able to:

- Know the basics of National Tourist Guide Accreditation Examination in China
- Understand how to apply for the National Tourist Guide Certificate and ID Card
- Understand competency standards and national qualifications for guides
- Know pre-qualification examination training and annual renewal or annual auditing training

Opening Case

National Tour Guide Accreditation Program of Australia

The National Tour Guide Accreditation Program of Australia is suitable for tourist guides in all sectors of the tourism industry and encourages professional development and promotes training in all relevant skills.

Guides of Australia accreditation program is owned and maintained by Guiding Organizations Australia Inc. (GOA). In the tour-guiding fields, there are 3 relevant certificates:

- Certificate III in Tourism (Guiding).
- Certificate IV in Tourism (Guiding).
- Certificate IV in Tourism (Natural and Cultural Heritage).

As a part of the accreditation process, you will undertake a "field evaluation" of your tour or activity. This consists of 2 elements — the 'Plan' and the 'Evaluation'.

As a part of the evaluation process you will need to submit a plan for the tour or activity you intend to conduct. A plan helps you to establish what you will talk about, when, and what props you will need along the way. It also helps you to tailor the tour or activity to the expected customer group.

The tour or activity field evaluation should be no less than 1 hour or an equivalent makeup, to allow sufficient time to show your skills. It is recommended that your tour or activity be conducted in a real on-the-job situation with no less than 2 customers plus the evaluator. If this is not possible, a simulated tour or activity reflecting real circumstances may be evaluated.

An evaluator will be assigned to you once your application is received and will contact you within 30 days. This evaluator will guide you through the accreditation process, take fees payment, arrange a time and conduct the field evaluation, and sign off on your accreditation. All evaluators are senior tour guides with one of Guiding Organizations Australia Inc member organizations, or an accepted external specialist, with an equivalent of 5 years experience as a tour guide, knowledge of tourism qualification requirements and experience in tour guide assessment. Your evaluator should be a person from outside of the tour operation/company at which you are employed/contracted. You can appeal the accreditation decision if you feel you have been treated unfairly or are not happy with the outcome. You should make a formal appeal in writing to Guiding Organizations Australia within 14 days of the decision or event. An independent evaluator will then be assigned to consult with you and the initial evaluator. The independent evaluator may need to conduct a second field evaluation.

(Source: http://www.goa.org.au/GuidesofAustralia.aspx.)

1. Who is eligible to take the National Tour Guide Accreditation Program of Australia?

2. What are the 3 relevant certificates of guides in Australia?

3. How to undertake a field evaluation?

4. What is your comment on the National Tour Guide Accreditation Program of Australia?

Qualification and Training | 59

Introduction

Whilst it was argued in chapter 3 that tourist guides are representatives of the cities, regions and countries for which they are qualified, in this chapter we will further discuss qualification, licensing, certification and training program for ensuring a quality guiding service in China.

4.1 Qualification

Since its launching in 1989, National Tourist Guide Accreditation Examination (NTGAE, 全国导游人员等级考核) has evolved and necessarily devolved over the years.

From 1989 to 2000, National Tourism Administration of The People's Republic of China (CNTA) was the leading examination *authority*, and the assessment took the form of written exams and, to a lesser extent, the *demonstration* of practical guiding skills. Since China is so large and with regions or provinces that have such a wide variety of tourism features and characteristics, the exam for Basic Knowledge of Tour Guiding was divided into two parts: one for general national level tour guiding knowledge and the other for more specific local tour guiding knowledge.

In 1990s, some provincial level tourism administrations began organizing a local level tourist guide qualification examination. This eventually became common practice at local levels. Thus, by the end of the 1990s, both national and local tourist guide qualification examination system was in operation.

From 2001 up to now, CNTA further decentralized some of its administrative functions including the tourist guide qualification examination. Under the new system, different provinces have developed different exams tailored to their own industry needs. As a result, exam content and the selection *criteria* are no longer *standardized* across the provinces and, as a result, local qualification certificate holders can only work in the province where they get their certificates (Huang and Weiler, 2010).

Qualification and Training

Knowledge Links [4-1]

> 国家旅游局组织设立全国导游人员等级考核评定委员会,并由全国导游人员等级考核评定委员会组织实施全国导游人员等级考核评定工作。省、自治区、直辖市和新疆生产建设兵团旅游行政管理部门组织设立导游人员等级考核证实办公室,在全国导游人员等级考核评定委员会的授权和指导下开展相应的工作。
>
> (资料来源:《导游人员等级考核评定管理办法(试行)》.)

Generally speaking, in adhere to the "*Regulations* on *Accreditation* of Tourist Guide (Draft) by Order No.22 of the CNTA (July 3, 2005)"(《导游人员等级考核评定管理办法(试行)》) and "Regulations on Management of Tourist Guide released by the CNTA (Oct.1, 1999)" (《导游人员管理条例》), CNTA has launched a national tourist guide accreditation program called NTGAE setting a skills benchmark for all tourist guides in China. The NTGAE is managed by National Tourist guide Accreditation Committee of China (NTGACC, 全国导游人员等级考核评定委员会), and Tourist Guide Accreditation Offices (TGAO, 导游人员等级考核证实办公室) are set up at provincial and *municipal* levels to ensure the *execution* of *ordinances* and orders from the NTGACC.

Knowledge Links [4-2]

> 我国实行全国统一的导游人员资格考试制度。具有高级中学、中等专业学校或者以上学历,身体健康,具有适应导游需要的基本知识和语言表达能力的中华人民共和国公民,可以参加导游人员资格考试;经考试合格的,由国务院旅游行政部门或者国务院旅游行政部门委托省、自治区、直辖市人民政府旅游行政部门颁发导游人员资格证书。
>
> (资料来源:《导游人员管理条例》.)

The application requirements for the NTGAE is as following.

- Abiding by the *constitution*, laws and ordinances, and sticking to the Party's Four *Cardinal* Principles of PRC.
- Holding a certificate of senior high school or *vocational* school, or above.
- Being in good health.
- With Basic knowledge and language skills required in guiding.
- Being a Chinese citizen, or permanent Chinese resident from Hong Kong or Macao.

Paper test is held on October annually, including 4 subjects for *candidates* of certificate, and the cost is about 180 Yuan(Table 4.1). Both Chinese and foreign language speaking candidates of *certificate* II will need to take a combined paper test with questions requiring short (single word or phrase) answers and questions requiring essay/note answers. The test involves 2 *modules*, namely, Knowledge on Travel and Tourism (导游知识专题), Chinese Literature (汉语言文学知识). For those foreign language speaking candidates, Chinese Literature will be replaced by the Chosen Language Ability Exam (外语). Although the test for candidates of certificate III are also paper based, the modules with the chosen languages have been changed to Case Study (导游案例分析) and Commentary Writing (导游词创作). As for certificate IV, the candidate will be required to write a paper or essay, and then present his findings on *seminar*.

Table 4.1 Paper test for NTGAE in Sichuan province

Subject	Scores
Knowledge of Tour Guiding (导游综合知识)	100 Points
Knowledge of Chinese Literature (导游汉语言文学知识)	50 Points
Regulations and Ordinances about Tourism (旅游政策与法规)	100 Points
Practical Skills in Tour Guiding (导游实务)	50 Points
Total	300 Points

Qualification and Training

You will need to complete and provide the following application documentations to participate in the oral test (Appendix Ⅰ).

- Application form — provided in Appendix Ⅱ.
- Examination admission card.
- 1 inch sized photo — the same one as uploaded in the TGAO's website.
- ID card.
- Current certificate or *diploma.*
- Health report — for Chinese-speaking tourist guide certificate applicants only.
- *Relevant*: Tour guiding qualifications and its certified copy — for Chinese-speaking tourist guide certificate holders applying for the second language certificate.

Knowledge Links [4-3]

> 四川省 2012 年全国导游人员资格考试笔试包括导游综合知识（100分）、导游汉语言文学知识（50分）、旅游政策与法规（100分）、四川导游实务（50分）4 科，总计 300 分。考试由省旅游局统一命题、统一制卷、统一评卷。各市、州旅游局负责本考区考务工作。试题均由客观题构成，考生填涂机读卡。除小语种考生外，其他考生的笔试成绩作为口试资格凭证，不带入口试计算总成绩。中文类口试包括模拟景点讲解（75分）、模拟途中讲解（75分）两科，总计 150 分。外语类口试包括模拟景点讲解（65分）、模拟途中讲解（65分）及口译（20分）3 科，总计 150 分。小语种考生根据笔试和口试的总成绩，统一划定合格分数线。
>
> 资料来源：《四川省旅游局关于组织 2012 年全国导游人员资格考试的通知》.)

Oral test commences on December annually. Chinese speaking tourist guide certificate applicants are required to pass all the 3 subjects (Table 4.2) and the cost is about 60 Yuan. For those foreign Language speaking tourist guide certificate applicants, all the 3 subjects are tested in chosen language like Japanese, Germany, French, Thai, or Korean. Besides, they are required to complete the following 3 sessions: a. Dialogue; b. Interpretation; c. Q&A (Table 4.3).

Table 4.2 Oral test in Chinese for NTGAE in Sichuan province

Subject	Scores
Commentary at a specific Site (模拟景点讲解)	55 Points
Guiding on a specific rout (模拟途中讲解)	55 Points
Language skill and etiquette (语言表达、仪表礼仪)	40 Points
Total	150 Points

Table 4.3 Oral test in foreign language for NTGAE in Sichuan province

Subject	Scores
Dialogue (命题会话)	20 Points
Interpretation (外汉互译)	20 Points
Q&A (文化知识问答)	10 Points
Total	50 Points

The Application fee for those who hold Chinese-speaking tourist guide certificate (or *equivalent*) and want to take oral test in a chosen foreign language, is about 25 Yuan. The paper test result along with *minimum* passing score is released by provincial tourism administration, normally on November, while oral test result along with minimum passing score is released about 2 months later. Applicants could visit the website of the local tourism administration to check the testing result. Both Chinese and English speaking tourist guide certificate applicants reaching the minimum passing score for paper test are *eligible* to take the oral test; meanwhile, all those foreign language speaking tourist guide certificate applicants excluding English speaking one are eligible to take the oral test, and the minimum passing score is based on *merit*, thus considering the number of participants.

4.2 Certification

NTGAE includes competency standards and national qualifications for guides. In the tour-guiding fields, there are 4 relevant certificates:
- Certificate I in Tour Guiding (Elementary Level).
- Certificate II in Tour Guiding (Intermediate Level).
- Certificate III in Tour Guiding (Advanced Level).
- Certificate IV in Tour Guiding (Expert Level).

Knowledge Links [4-4]

> 导游人员分为初级、中级、高级、特级4个等级。初级导游和中级导游考核由省级旅游行政管理部门或其委托的地市级旅游行政管理部门组织评定；高级导游和特级导游由国务院旅游行政管理部门组织评定。
>
> 导游员申报等级时，由低到高，逐级递升，经考核评定合格者，颁发相应的导游员等级证书。中级导游员的考核采取笔试方式。其中，中文导游人员考试科目为"导游知识专题"和"汉语言文学知识"；外语导游人员考试科目为"导游知识专题"和"外语"。高级导游员的考核采取笔试方式，考试科目为"导游案例分析"和"导游词创作"。特级导游员的考核采取论文答辩方式。参加省部级以上单位组织的导游技能大赛获得最佳名次的导游人员，报全国导游人员等级考核评定委员会批准后，可晋升一级导游人员等级。一人多次获奖只能晋升一次，晋升的最高等级为高级。
>
> （资料来源：《导游人员等级考核评定管理办法（试行）》.）

After passing the qualification examination, an individual is treated as an elementary tour guide and can only be promoted one level at a time through evaluation and assessment organized by the tourism authorities. Written examinations must be taken in order to progress to a higher level, and for the supreme level tour guides, a thesis examination with an oral defense is required. For their understanding of being required to perform as a guide at a higher level and therefore enhance their capacity to contribute to sustainable tourism, they are examined for their understanding of thematic knowledge in religion, architecture, food culture, martial arts, Chinese medicine, Chinese language & literature, and tour guiding script writing (Huang and Weiler, 2010).

4.3 Licensing

Tourist guide licensing in China is separated from the qualification examination process, although the latter is closely related to licensing and serves as the preparation stage for it. Tourist guides in China must secure a license before working legally in the profession, and it has considerable potential as a mechanism for quality assurance.

Knowledge Links [4-5]

> 取得导游人员资格证书的，经与旅行社订立劳动合同或者在导游服务公司登记，方可持所订立的劳动合同或者登记证明材料，向省、自治区、直辖市人民政府旅游行政部门申请领取导游证。具有特定语种语言能力的人员，虽未取得导游人员资格证书，在旅行社需要聘请临时从事

> 导游活动的人员时，可由旅行社向省、自治区、直辖市人民政府旅游行政部门申请领取临时导游证。
>
> 　　有下列情形之一的，不得颁发导游证：①无民事行为能力或者限制民事行为能力的；②患有传染性疾病的；③受过刑事处罚、过失犯罪的除外；④被吊销导游证的。
>
> （资料来源：《导游人员管理条例》．）

Individuals who have obtained a tourist guide qualification certificate can apply for a tourist guide license at provincial level tourism administrations after registering themselves with a tour guiding services company or signing an employment contract with a travel agency. Since 2002, different colors are used to depict the professional classification level of the guide. The new model license certificate integrates intelligence card (IC) technology, with a metal **SIM card** storing digital information about the license holder including name, gender, ethnicity, education level, working language, date of birth, home address, personal identification number, license number and tour guide qualification certificate number (Huang and Weiler, 2010).

Therefore, upon successful completion of all accreditation requirements, ID card will be produced to identify you as an accredited tourist guide with the travel agency or company that you are representing in China.

You will need to complete and provide the following application documentations to the local tourism administration at respective provincial or municipal levels.

- Relevant tour guiding qualifications and its certified copy.
- Contract with travel company and its certified copy.
- ID card and its certified copy.
- Application form.

Once you receive your ID card, keep it with you when guiding, others can identify you as accredited, particularly tourists and others in the industry. Tourist guides must take a license certificate when conducting any tour guiding activities.

Knowledge Links [4-6]

> 新版导游证（2002年版）为IC卡形式，可借助读卡机查阅卡中存储的导游基本情况和违规计分情况等信息，导游证的正面设置中英文对照的"导游证（China tour guide）"、导游证等级、编号、姓名、语种等项目，中间为持证人近期免冠2英寸正面照片，导游证等级以4种不同的颜色加以区分：初级为灰色、中级为粉米色、高级为淡黄色、特级为金黄色；背面印有注意事项和卡号。导游证的编号规则为"D-0000-000000"，英文字母"D"为"导"字的拼音字母的缩写，代表导游，前4位数字为省、城市、地区的标准国际代码，后6位数字为计数编码。不同等级的导游证卡号依各自的顺序编号。
>
> （资料来源：《导游证管理办法》.）

4.4 Training

CNTA has a dedicated division of education and training that regards tourist guide training as one of its most prominent responsibilities. CNTA formulates training policies and plans, but seldom directly organizes training sessions for tourist guides. In addition to making relevant training policies, it does organize training sessions in relation to tour guiding training, for instance, "training the trainers" programme targeting major regional tourist guide trainers, or training sessions familiarizing local tourist guide examination officers with new policies.

Knowledge Links [4-7]

> 国家对导游人员实行年度审核制度，导游人员必须参加年审。国务院旅游行政管理部门负责制定全国导游人员年审工作政策，组织实施并监督检查。省级旅游行政管理部门负责组织、指导本行政区域内导游人员的年审工作并监督检查。所在地旅游行政管理部门具体负责组织实施对导游人员的年审工作。年审以考评为主，考评的内容应包括当年从事导游业务情况、扣分情况、接受行政处罚情况、游客反映情况等。考评等级为通过年审、暂缓通过年审和不予通过年审3种。
>
> （资料来源：《导游人员等级考核评定管理办法（试行）》.）

At provincial and city levels, most tourism administrations have an industry-training centre affiliated with them. These training centers play a major role in many kinds of local tourist guide training programme. Many universities with tourism programme also receive contracted tourist guide training from local tourism authorities or organize independent training courses, mostly targeting pre-qualification examination training. A number of private profit-making training schools also undertake pre-qualification examination training as their core business. These training activities include pre-qualification examination training and annual renewal or annual auditing training (Huang and Weiler, 2010).

The annual renewal is for continuous professional development (CPD), which provides the way of updating and expanding knowledge, and of further developing skills, so as to meet this objective that qualified tourist guides have a professional duty to ensure that they consistently offer the highest quality of guiding services to customers. It is essential that all the working tourist guides undertake and keep a record of the annual renewal. Only in this way will tourist guides demonstrate commitment to sustain assured levels of guiding competence. In order to maintain the accreditation, tourist guides must undertake professional development annually.

In December of each year a notice will be sent to you via email or SMS and you may also check the "annual renewal" information at the website of the Tourism Administration Office. To ensure continuation of your registration and ID card, you will be asked to return the card back to the Tourism Administration Office and audit some lectures. The ID card will be given back to you soon after the annual renewal is completed.

The annual renewal lasts about 1 week or no less than 56 hours per annum. The training content comprises political ideology and professional ethics, updates on policies and regulations, tour guiding business knowledge and skills. CNTA strongly advocates that all tourism enterprises that employ tourist guides run on-the-job training and low-season training for tourist guides.

Summary

Summary

This chapter provides a brief view of qualification and training programme for tourist guides in China.

In terms of competency standards, there are 4 levels of relevant certificates. Participants on National Tour Guide Accreditation Examination launched by CNTA must pass all elements of both paper and oral examinations at the relevant level before they receive their certificates. Lastly, this chapter also introduces the annual renewal programme for Chinese tourist guides to maintain their accreditation.

Key Words and Phrases

Authority /ɔːˈθɒriti/ *noun*: a government organization that has control of a specified activity or area.

Demonstration /ˌdemənˈstreɪʃ(ə)n/ *noun*: an act of showing someone how something is used or done.

Decentralize /diˈsentrəˌlaiz/ *verb*: to change (something) by taking control, power, etc., from one person or group and giving it to many people or groups throughout an area.

Criteria /kraiˈtiriə/ *noun*: (plural form of criterion): something that is used as a reason for making a judgment or decision.

Standardize /ˈstændəˌdaiz/ *verb*: to change (things) so that they are similar and consistent and agree with rules about what is proper and acceptable.

Regulation /ˌregjuˈleɪʃ(ə)n/ *noun*: an official rule or law that says how something should be done.

Accreditation /əˌkrediˈteɪʃ(ə)n/ *noun*: the act of attesting and approval as meeting a prescribed standard.

Municipal /mjuˈnisip(ə)l/ *adjective*: of or relating to the government of a city or town.

Execution /ˌeksiˈkjuːʃ(ə)n/ *noun*: the act of doing or performing something.

Ordinance /ˈɔːdinins/ *noun*: a law or regulation made by a city or town government.

Constitution /ˌkɒnstiˈtjuːʃ(ə)n/ *noun*: the system of beliefs and laws by which a country, state, or organization is governed.

Cardinal /ˈkɑːdin(ə)l/ *noun*: of foremost importance; paramount.

Vocational /vəuˈkeiʃ(ə)n(ə)l/ *adjective*: relating to the special skills, training, etc., that you need for a particular job or occupation.

Candidate /ˈkændiˌdeit, -dət/ *noun*: a person who is trying to be elected.

Certificate /səˈtifikət/ *noun*: a document that is official proof that something has happened.

Module /ˈmɔdjuːl/ *noun*: one of a set of parts that can be connected or combined to build or complete something.

Seminar/ˈsemiˌnɑː/ *noun*: a meeting in which you receive information and training in a particular subject.

Diploma /diˈpləumə/ *noun*: a document which shows that a person has finished a course of study or has graduated from a school.

Relevant /ˈreliv(ə)nt/ *adjective*: relating to a subject in an appropriate way.

Equivalent /iˈkwivələnt/ *noun*: something that has the same value, use, meaning, etc., as another thing.

Minimum /ˈminiməm/ *adjective*: least or lowest possible in amount or degree.

Eligible /ˈelidʒib(ə)l/ *adjective*: able to be chosen for something; able to do or receive something.

Merit /ˈmerit/ *noun*: a good quality or feature that deserves to be praised.

SIM Card: 用户识别卡

Qualification and Training

Review Questions

1. What does NTGAE stand for?
2. Compare the differences between guide certificates in China and UK.
3. How to participate on the NTGAE?
4. Are you willing to take part in the NTGAE and how will you get prepared for it?

Choice Questions

Choose the best answer to the questions below. You need to correctly answer 3 of the 5 questions to pass.

1. In adhere to the "Regulations on Accreditation of Tourist Guide (Draft) by Order No.22 of the CNTA, which organ is responsible for managing the NTGAE?

   A. National Tourism Administration of the People's Republic of China

   B. Tourist Guide Accreditation Offices

   C. Provincial Tourism Administration

   D. National Tourist Guide Accreditation Committee of China

2. Which one is not the application requirement for NTGAE?

   A. Holding a certificate of senior high school or vocational school, or above

   B. Being in good health

   C. Being a Chinese citizen, or permanent Chinese resident from Hong Kong or Macao

   D. Holding a certificate of the chosen language like CET-4

3. Which application documentations is not correctly prepared for participating in the Oral test:

   A. 5 inches sized photo

   B. Application form

C. Health report

D. Current certificate or diploma

4. If you hold a Certificate II in tour guiding (Intermediate Level) and apply for Certificate III, which subjects are you supposed to take?

   A. Knowledge of Tour Guiding; Knowledge of Chinese Literature; Regulations and Ordinances about Tourism; Practical Skills in Tour Guiding

   B. Knowledge on Travel and Tourism; and Chinese Literature

   C. To write a paper or essay, and present the findings on seminar

   D. Case Study; and Commentary Writing

5. Individuals who have obtained a tourist guide qualification certificate can apply for a tourist guide license to provincial level tourism administrations after registering themselves with a tour guiding services company or signing an employment contract with a travel agency.

   A. True
   B. False

Group Discussion

China's national standard for tour guiding practice, its examination process, and its licensing and registration process are all legal requirements to the practice as a tour guide. These in turn lay the groundwork for enforcing minimum tour guiding standards across the industry.

However, China's quality assurance system for tour guiding is not perfect, as there is weakness for further improvement. A good case in point is that China's system both for achieving minimum standards and for rewarding excellence largely neglects a number of the tour guiding roles, especially those roles as tour leading, managing the tour in time and space, managing the health and safety of the group, compliance with legal and ethical standards, and providing government-endorsed information and basic customer service.

(Source: Huang. S, Weiler B. A review and evaluation of China's quality assurance system for tour guiding. Journal of Sustainable Tourism. 2010, 18 (7): 845–860.)

Qualification and Training

- Would you please further discuss the advantages as well as disadvantages of China's quality assurance system for tour guiding?
- Would you point out some suggestions for improving this system?

Guiding Exercise

The group arrives at the Inter Continental Hotel, Shanghai. While the bellboy is handling the baggage and tourists are all resting in the lobby, you are supposed to briefly introduce the hotel to the tourists.

After Jason, the tour leader, collects all the passports, it is your duty to help them check in and set morning call. Firstly, you need to show to the receptionist all the necessary files like name list, passports, schedule, and booking receipt (if there is one). As soon as rooms are booked, please give room cards to the tour leader who is to dispatch the card to the tourists. You should discuss the time for tomorrow's departure with him before you set morning call. Then, please make sure that bellmen take the right luggage to the right room. Last but not the least, please say goodbye to the tourists and wish them have a pleasant stay.

Translation Exercise

1. Please translate the following passage into Chinese.

The Chinese government and the tourism industry have increasingly recognized the important role that tour guides play in the entire tourism system. Many of them have been working on ways to enhance the level of service quality and professionalism of the guiding profession, two factors widely regarded as highly critical in affecting tour guide performances.

2. Please translate the following passage into English.

导游资格考试是影响导游队伍素质的重要因素，要通过改革和完善导游资格考试，加强考试内容与导游从业能力的结合。旅行社和导游服务管理中心等依托机构要加强对导游的岗前培训，提高各语种导游、景区点导游、文博科教场馆讲解员的岗位服务技能。

Case Study

蒋先生参加了某旅行社组织的旅游团前往黄山旅游。临行前接受组团社的推荐，购买了旅游意外保险。在乘车前往的途中，汽车窗的玻璃突然被一块飞来的石头击碎，玻璃碎片将靠窗而坐的蒋先生扎伤。事后，蒋先生向旅行社索赔。旅行社说，此事故纯属意外，不是旅行社的责任，蒋先生应向保险公司索要旅游意外保险赔偿。但保险公司却认为，旅客在汽车上发生意外，应由旅游汽车公司负责赔偿。

1. 蒋先生到底应该向谁要求赔偿？为什么？
2. 对蒋先生的意外伤害，旅行社有无责任？为什么？

Further Reading

Professional Blue Badge tourist guides began to be trained in London after World War II in response to a demand for visitors wanting bomb site tours.

Participants on tourist guiding accredited programmes must pass all elements of the institute examinations at the relevant level before they receive their certificates (at Level 2) and their badges and certificates (at Level 3—Green Badge and Level 4—Blue Badge)

Candidates at Level 4 are entitled to 3 consecutive attempts (first and two resits) at their examinations to be completed within 36 months from the end of their training programme.

Candidates at Level 3 and Level 2 are entitled to 2 consecutive attempts (first and one resit) at their examinations to be completed within 24 months from the end of their training programme.

Blue Badge guides in Scotland are trained at university level and undergo an intensive two year part time training course amounting to 1 300 hours and involving weekend and summer school attendance at the University Edinburgh and in the field throughout the county.

Qualification and Training

In England, Wales, Northern Ireland and Jersey, Blue Badge guides are trained under the auspices of the Institute of Tourist Guiding (ITG), often in conjunction with universities or colleges of further education. Most training courses for guides last at least two academic terms and some, e.g. London, may be up to nearly 2 years. A wide spectrum of academic, specialist and practical training is covered as well as a core curriculum of the history, architecture and social development of the country.

Undoubtedly, some of the work that guides get asked to do around the country is traditional tourist guiding e.g. city tours by coach, guiding around cathedrals, castles and other heritage sites. There is also firm support for walking tours, not only from visitors but also locals.

Many guides are experts in a field and. will specialize in guiding art galleries or work primarily for groups like National Association of Decorative and Fine Arts Societies. Some guides are architects and will concentrate on architectural tours. Some are antiques experts and will be engaged by visitors with a similar interest.

Another area where there is a lot of expertise (and enthusiasm) is in sport. Wimbledon Tennis Club uses Blue Badge guides for their award winning tours. There are also over 250 multi-lingual guides who have taken a course specializing in the Olympic Games in order to be able to show visitors what is happening in London and around the country for the 2012 Games.

Prestigious museums and sites of national interest will only use Blue Badge tourist guides for their visitors e.g. London Blue Badge guides do the highlights tours for the British Museum and Parliament summer opening.

An increasing number of Blue Badge guides are licensed driver guides offering personalized chauffeur-driven guiding. Their work can vary from antiques tours in the Cotswolds, to looking after foreign journalists and film stars.

Blue Badge tourist guides are frequently used by destination management companies or DMCs to work with their corporate clients on large programmes. Sometimes this work will involve guiding excursions, but often it requires guides to take on the role of a knowledgeable local friend.

Many guides are fluent in more than one language. Indeed, many guides are not native English speakers and work in their own mother tongue e.g. Chinese Mandarin, Russian, or Japanese.

Apart from guiding, some Blue Badge guides work directly for large companies, creating and operating programmes for conferences, incentive tours and training seminars. Others are involved in training and not only guide training, but for example, teaching presentational skills to personnel in industry. Some run their own lecture courses.

The Green Badge guide is Level 3 equivalent (e.g. city of London). If you are interested in working full or part-time guiding visitors round an area such as a city or town centre or in a site like a visitor attraction, historic building or heritage resource, then this qualification is for you.

You will have a qualification enabling you to:
- Offer flexible route walking tours in a specified area as above.
- Guide in 2 contrasting environments (both exterior and interior).
- Have an in-depth knowledge of your specified area.
- Have a range of communication skills essential for the delivery of an effective commentary and presentation.

Exceptionally the qualification could cover one flexible route tour on foot and one fixed route coach tour or similar.

On completion you will be assessed with 1 written and 2 practical examinations. You will also be tested on your ability to plan a tour on foot to meet the particular needs of a given group of visitors.

This qualification will provide you with the foundation for progression to Level 4 and the Blue Badge. As a successful candidate at this level you will be eligible to apply to join the Institute as an Associate.

Certificates-Level 2 is for those who are thinking of entering the tourism industry to take up paid or voluntary employment guiding visitors round an attraction such as a stately home, cathedral, museum or theme park, or perhaps a business or industrial site. You will have a qualification enabling you to:
- Offer fixed route tours on foot in a specified site, or exceptionally on a moving vehicle like a boat or open-top bus.

Qualification and Training

- Have an in-depth knowledge of your site.
- Have a range of communication skills essential for the delivery of an effective commentary and presentation.

The institute accredited course is quite demanding, with 50~70 contact hours (time attending lectures or practical sessions on site) and in addition some 120 hours of private study. Courses are usually run when there is a demand for guides in a particular area, by local and regional tourist bodies or colleges and institutions. They are part-time, with evening lectures and practical training at weekends, so you can qualify while still doing a full-time job. On completion you will be assessed with one written and two practical examinations. You will also be tested on your ability to plan a tour on foot to meet the particular needs of a given group of visitors.

(Source: http://www.itg.org.uk.)

Chapter 5
Legal and Ethical Issues in Tour Guiding

Learning Outcomes

After reading this chapter, you will be able to:

- Understand legal requirements in tour guiding
- Recognize the code of guiding practice
- Be aware of the ethical obligations of tourist guides

Opening Case

The Travel Industry Council of Hong Kong (TIC) announced at 8 November, 2006 that the tourist guide who had recently abandoned a tour group from Qinghai province was suspended by the Tourist Guide Deliberation Committee for three months, and the travel agent being responsible for providing reception services for the tour group was fined HK$100 000 and its membership was suspended for one month on probation for six months by the compliance committee. In view of the seriousness of the case, the committee found that tourist guides shall always have regard for the interests of visitors and the reputation of the Hong Kong tourism industry, and that tourist guides shall not coerce or mislead visitors into making purchases.

Mr. Joseph Tung, executive director of the TIC, stressed, "The Tourist Guide Deliberation Committee was of the view that although the tourist guide admitted his own mistake, this incident not only affected the interests of the tour group, but also damaged the reputation of Hong Kong and Hong Kong tourism and gravely affected the industry. The Committee therefore decided to suspend his "pass" for 3 months. I hope all tourist guides will learn a lesson from this incident."

1. What is your comment on the improper behavior of the tourist guide who abandoned a tour group from Qinghai province?

2. What can you learn from this incident?

Chapter 5

Introduction

Tourist guides need to be aware of legislation and ethical code guiding their profession. In this chapter, we will briefly discuss laws, regulations, rules and standards in broad areas, as well as code of conduct and ethical obligations for tour guiding.

Legal and Ethical Issues in Tour Guiding

5.1 Legal Requirement

For our professional career as tourist guides, we will be considering and applying certain aspects of the following laws, regulations, rules and standards for tour guiding services.

5.1.1 Laws

- *Passport Law of the People's Republic of China* (《中华人民共和国护照法》).
- *Food Hygiene Law of the People's Republic of China* (《中华人民共和国食品卫生法》).
- *Interim Measures of the National Tourism Administration on the Implementation of Administrative License by Order No.27 of the National Tourism Administration* (《国家旅游局行政许可实施暂行办法》).
- *Regulations on "Procuring Insurance of Travel Agencies" Liability by Order No.35 of the National Tourism Administration* [《旅行社责任保险管理办法》]
- *Regulations of the People's Republic of China on Frontier Inspection of Exit from or Entry into the Country* (《中华人民共和国出境入境边防检查条例》).

Knowledge Links[5-1]

旅行社责任保险的保险责任，应当包括旅行社在组织旅游活动中依法对旅游者的人身伤亡、财产损失承担的赔偿责任和依法对受旅行社委派并为旅游者提供服务的导游或者领队人员的人身伤亡承担的赔偿责任。具体包括下列情形：①因旅行社疏忽或过失应当承担赔偿责任的；②因发生意外事故旅行社应当承担赔偿责任的；③国家旅游局会同中国保险监督管理委员会(以下简称中国保监会)规定的其他情形。

旅行社责任保险的保险期间为 1 年。责任限额可以根据旅行社业务经营范围、经营规模、风险管控能力、当地经济社会发展水平和旅行社自身需要，由旅行社与保险公司协商确定，但每人人身伤亡责任限额不得低于 20 万元人民币。

（资料来源：《旅行社责任保险管理办法》.）

5.1.2 Regulations

- *Regulations on Tourism Agencies (May 1, 2009)* (《旅行社条例》).

Knowledge Links [5-2]

旅行社是指从事招徕、组织、接待旅游者等活动，为旅游者提供相关旅游服务，开展国内旅游业务、入境旅游业务或者出境旅游业务的企业法人。申请设立旅行社，经营国内旅游业务和入境旅游业务的，应当有固定的经营场所，有必要的营业设施，有不少于 30 万元的注册资本。旅行社分社的设立不受地域限制，其经营范围不得超出设立分社的旅行社的经营范围。旅行社服务网点应当接受旅行社的统一管理，不得从事招徕、咨询以外的活动。

经营国内旅游业务和入境旅游业务的旅行社，应当存入质量保证金 20 万元；经营出境旅游业务的旅行社，应当增存质量保证金 120 万元。质量保证金的利息属于旅行社所有。旅行社每设立一个经营国内旅游业务和入境旅游业务的分社，应当向其质量保证金账户增存 5 万元；每设立一个经营出境旅游业务的分社，应当向其质量保证金账户增存 30 万元。

（资料来源：《旅行社条例》.）

Legal and Ethical Issues in Tour Guiding

- *CNTA Order No. 30: Detailed Rules for the Implementation of the Tourism Agencies Regulations to Become Effective as of 3 May 2009* (《旅行社条例实施细则》).

Knowledge Links [5-3]

> 擅自引进外商投资、设立服务网点未在规定期限内备案，或者旅行社及其分社、服务网点未悬挂旅行社业务经营许可证、备案登记证明的，由县级以上旅游行政管理部门责令改正，可以处 1 万元以下的罚款。
>
> 旅行社为接待旅游者选择的交通、住宿、餐饮、景区等企业，不具有合法经营资格或者接待服务能力的，由县级以上旅游行政管理部门责令改正，没收违法所得，处违法所得 3 倍以下但最高不超过 3 万元的罚款，没有违法所得的，处 1 万元以下的罚款。
>
> 要求旅游者必须参加旅行社安排的购物活动、需要旅游者另行付费的旅游项目，或者对同一旅游团队的旅游者提出与其他旅游者不同合同事项的，由县级以上旅游行政管理部门责令改正，处 1 万元以下的罚款。
>
> （资料来源：《旅行社条例实施细则》.）

- *Supplementary Regulations on Interim Provisions on the Establishment of Foreign-Controlled and Wholly Foreign-Funded Travel Agencies by Order No.25 of the National Tourism Administration* (《设立外商控股、外商独资旅行社暂行规定》的补充规定).
- *Amendment of the Interim Provisions on the Establishment of Foreign-Controlled and Wholly Foreign-Funded Travel Agencies by Order No. 20 of the National Tourism Administration* (对《设立外商控股、外商独资旅行社暂行规定》的修订).
- *Regulations on Management of Tourist Guide released by the CNTA* (《导游人员管理条例》).

Knowledge Links [5-4]

　　导游人员进行导游活动时,应当佩戴导游证,必须经旅行社委派,不得私自承揽或者以其他任何方式直接承揽导游业务。未佩戴导游证带团的,由旅游行政部门责令改正;拒不改正的,处 500 元以下的罚款。无导游证进行导游活动的,由旅游行政部门责令改正并予以公告,处 1 000 元以上 3 万元以下的罚款;有违法所得的,并处没收违法所得。未经旅行社委派,私自承揽或者以其他任何方式直接承揽导游业务,进行导游活动的,由旅游行政部门责令改正,处 1 000 元以上 3 万元以下的罚款;有违法所得的,并处没收违法所得;情节严重的,由省、自治区、直辖市人民政府旅游行政部门吊销导游证并予以公告。

　　对于导游人员有损害国家利益和民族尊严的言行的,由旅游行政部门责令改正;情节严重的,由省、自治区、直辖市人民政府旅游行政部门吊销导游证并予以公告;对该导游人员所在的旅行社给予警告直至责令停业整顿。

　　导游人员应当严格按照旅行社确定的接待计划,安排旅游者的旅行、游览活动,不得擅自增加、减少旅游项目或者中止导游活动。遇有可能危及旅游者人身安全的紧急情形时,经征得多数旅游者的同意,可以调整或者变更接待计划,但是应当立即报告旅行社。对于擅自增加或者减少旅游项目,擅自变更接待计划,擅自中止导游活动的,由旅游行政部门责令改正,暂扣导游证 3～6 个月;情节严重的,由省、自治区、直辖市人民政府旅游行政部门吊销导游证并予以公告。

　　导游人员在引导旅游者旅行、游览过程中,应当就可能发生危及旅游者人身、财物安全的情况,向旅游者作出真实说明和明确警示,并按照旅行社的要求采取防止危害发生的措施;不得向旅游者兜售物品或者购买旅游者的物品,不得以明示或者暗示的方式向旅游者索要小费;不得欺骗、胁迫旅游者消费或者与经营者串通欺骗、胁迫旅游者消费。向旅游者兜售物品或者购买旅游者的物品的,或者以明示或者暗示的方式向旅游者索要小费的,由旅游行政部门责令改正,处 1 000 元以上 3 万元

Legal and Ethical Issues in Tour Guiding

> 以下的罚款；有违法所得的，并处没收违法所得；情节严重的，由省、自治区、直辖市人民政府旅游行政部门吊销导游证并予以公告；对委派该导游人员的旅行社给予警告直至责令停业整顿。
>
> 　　导游人员进行导游活动，欺骗、胁迫旅游者消费或者与经营者串通欺骗、胁迫旅游者消费的，由旅游行政部门责令改正，处1 000元以上3万元以下的罚款；有违法所得的，并处没收违法所得；情节严重的，由省、自治区、直辖市人民政府旅游行政部门吊销导游证并予以公告；对委派该导游人员的旅行社给予警告直至责令停业整顿；构成犯罪的，依法追究刑事责任。
>
> （资料来源：《导游人员管理条例》.）

- *Detailed Rules for Implementation of Regulations on Management of Tourist Guide by Order No.15 of CNTA* (《导游人员管理实施办法》).

Knowledge Links [5-5]

> 　　导游人员计分办法实行年度10分制。导游人员10分分值被扣完后，由最后扣分的旅游行政执法单位暂时保留其导游证，并出具保留导游证证明，并于10日内通报导游人员所在地旅游行政管理部门和登记注册单位。正在带团过程中的导游人员，可持旅游执法单位出具的保留证明完成团队剩余行程。对导游人员的违法、违规行为除扣减其相应分值外，依法应予处罚的，依据有关法律给予处罚。导游人员通过年审后，年审单位应核销其遗留分值，重新输入初始分值。
>
> （资料来源：《导游人员管理实施办法》.）

- *Regulations on Accreditation of Tourist Guide (Draft) by Order No.22 of the CNTA* (《导游人员等级考核评定管理办法(试行)》).
- *The Administrative Measures of the Customs of the People's Republic of China for the Inspection of Imported and Exported Goods* (《中华人民共和国海关进出口货物查验管理办法》)

- *Regulations of the Customs of People's Republic of China on the Administration of Luggage and Articles Carried by Transit Passengers* (《中华人民共和国海关关于过境旅客行李物品管理规定》).

- *Interim Provisions on Import Taxes on Articles Taken Into China by Foreigners Permanently Residing in China* (《外国在华常驻人员携带进境物品进口税收暂行规定》).

- *Regulations of the Customs of People's Republic of China on the Administration of Self-used Articles Carried by Inbound and Outbound Passengers* (《中华人民共和国海关对进出境旅客旅行自用物品的管理规定》).

- *Regulations of the Customs of People's Republic of China on the Clearance of Inbound and Outbound Passengers* (《中华人民共和国海关关于进出境旅客通关的规定》).

- *Interim Provisions Concerning* **Compensation** *for Bodily Injury of Passengers in Domestic Air Transport* (《国内航空运输旅客身体损害赔偿暂行规定》).

- *Regulations of the Customs of the People's Republic of China on the Control of Inbound and Outbound Luggage and Articles Carried by Chinese Passengers* (《中华人民共和国海关对中国籍旅客进出境行李物品的管理规定》).

5.1.3 Rules/Standards

- *General Rules for Tourism Planning* (GB/T 18971—2003《旅游规划通则》).

- *Classification, Investigation and Evaluation of Tourism Resources* (GB/T 18972—2003) (《旅游资源分类、调查与评价》).

- *Basic Terms of Service in Tourism* (GB/T 16766-2010) [《旅游服务基础术语》(GB/T 16766-2010)].

Legal and Ethical Issues in Tour Guiding

- *Outbound Tour Service Quality of International Travel Agency*(LB/T 005—2002,《旅行社出境旅游服务质量》).
- *Tour Service Quality of Domestic Travel Agency*(LB/T 004—1997)《旅行社国内旅游服务质量要求》).
- *Service Quality of Tourist Coach*(LB/T 002—1995《旅游汽车服务质量》).
- *Classification and Evaluation of Tourism Toilets*(GB/T 18973－2003《旅游厕所质量等级的划分与评定》).
- *Specifications of Tour-Guide Service* (GB/T 15971—2010《导游服务规范》).

5.2 Code of Practice

"The code of practice" is defined as: "written guidelines issued by an official body or a professional association to its members to help them comply with its ethical standards". A code of practice is not a law, but it should be followed unless there is an alternative course of action that achieves the same or better standards.

Adherence to the **code of guiding practice** in China, a professional tourist guide provides an assurance of high level professionalism and a value-added service to their clients. He or she is supposed to demonstrate the tourist guides' code of guiding practice in his/her own actions and encourage its implementation across the industry through interactions with tourism businesses, organizations and other tourist guides. The code of guiding practice is manifested as the following principles and aims:

- To provide professional service to visitors, professional in care and commitment, and professional in providing an objective understanding of the place visited, free from *prejudice* or *propaganda*.
- To ensure that as far as possible what is presented as fact is true, and that a clear distinction is made between this truth and stories, legends, traditions, or opinions.
- To act honestly, fairly, professionally and reasonable in all dealings with all those who engage the services of guides and with colleagues working in all aspects of tourism.
- To protect the reputation of tourism in our country by making every endeavor to ensure that guided groups treat with respect to the environment, wildlife, sights and monuments, and also local customs and sensitivities.
- As representatives of the host country to welcome visitors and act in such a way, as to bring credit to the country visited and promote it as a tourist destination.
- Regularly update and upgrade guiding skills and knowledge through training and professional development activities.
- To declare to customers any relevant personal commercial interests, including *commissions*, and never force visitor to purchase or *solicit* tips.
- To be mindful at all times of duty of care and other health and safety issues.
- To provide all goods and services as presented in the tour itinerary and promotional material.
- To abide by all national, state or local legislation governing the operation and conduct of tours, tour operators and tourist guides.

Legal and Ethical Issues in Tour Guiding

Knowledge Links [5-6]

　　导游人员在导游活动中有下列情形之一的，扣除 10 分：有损害国家利益和民族尊严的言行的；诱导或安排旅游者参加黄、赌、毒活动项目的；有殴打或谩骂旅游者行为的；欺骗、胁迫旅游者消费的；未通过年审继续从事导游业务的；因自身原因造成旅游团重大危害和损失的。

　　导游人员在导游活动中有下列情形之一的，扣除 8 分：拒绝、逃避检查，或者欺骗检查人员的；擅自增加或者减少旅游项目的；擅自终止导游活动的；讲解中掺杂庸俗、下流、迷信内容的；未经旅行社委派私自承揽或者以其他任何方式直接承揽导游业务的。

　　导游人员在导游活动中有下列情形之一的，扣除 6 分：向旅游者兜售物品或购买旅游者物品的；以明示或者暗示的方式向旅游者索要小费的；因自身原因漏接漏送或误接误送旅游团的；讲解质量差或不讲解的；私自转借导游证供他人使用的；发生重大安全事故不积极配合有关部门救助的。

　　导游人员在导游活动中有下列情形之一的，扣除 4 分：私自带人随团游览的；无故不随团活动的；在导游活动中未佩带导游证或未携带计分卡；不尊重旅游者宗教信仰和民族风俗。

　　导游人员在导游活动中有下列情形之一的，扣除 2 分：未按规定时间到岗的；10 人以上团队未打接待社社旗的；未携带正规接待计划；接站未出示旅行社标识的；仪表、着装不整洁的；讲解中吸烟、吃东西的。

　　　　　　　　　　　（资料来源：《导游人员管理实施办法》.）

5.3 Ethical Obligations

The past experiences have clearly proved that the healthy development of China's tourism industry would largely rely on the good conduct of its tourist guides. It is of great significance to have all the tourist guides pass holders as well as future guides understood "dos and don'ts"; otherwise, misbehavior of tourist guides would not only ruin the reputation and future career of him/her, but also destroy the fragile tourist industry of China.

The ethics for guiding practice can go a long way in highlighting the need for displaying honesty and *integrity*, selflessness and *objectivity* in their dealings with tourists or customers.

A tourist guide needs to understand that his/her customer is buying a service. Not only is there a legal responsibility when taking someone's money, but there are principles for protection from liable by providing what is promised. The following is the fundamentals of being ethical:

- To provide a skilled presentation of knowledge, interpret and highlight surrounding, and inform and maintain objectivity and *enthusiasm* in an engaging manner.
- To be prepared for each tour when the itinerary is furnished in advance. A professional guide assumes responsibility for reporting on time and for meeting appointments and schedules within the guide's control. Be

Legal and Ethical Issues in Tour Guiding

sensitive to the interests and values of the tour group and not share his/her personal views on controversial subjects such as sex, religion, and politics.

- To have a wide range of knowledge of the city including its history and architecture, cultural and political life, and local folklore. Keep current on new exhibits, seasonal events, and other changes throughout the city. A professional guide does not knowingly give out misinformation.

- To follow the rules and regulations at all sites and facilities where he/she takes visitors.

- To know and follow the policies of the company. A guide does not accept or solicit a job from a client of the company that has hired him/her without the consent of the company. Therefore, personal business cards should not be distributed for these purposes. All business-related communication with the client should be made through the company only.

- To be knowledgeable about the best routes for all tours. This includes familiarity with the traffic laws. A professional guide informs the driver of the route in a calm, polite, and timely fashion.

- Dresses appropriately for the type of tour being conducted.

- To accept each tour as a serious commitment and cancels only when absolutely necessary and provides as much advance notice as possible.

- Does not solicit gratuities.

- Does not initiate patronization of souvenir shops and other places that practice "kickback" payments to the guide and/or drivers, or abuse *complimentary* meal privileges offered by food establishments.

- To cooperate with other tour groups and maintains ethical and professional

conduct at all times, cultivating a positive relationship with all colleagues.
- To respect the research and intellectual property of other guides and does not plagiarize or take as one's own another guide's commentary or individual presentation technique.

Legal and Ethical Issues in Tour Guiding | 95

Summary

Summary

The past experiences have clearly proved that the healthy development of China's tourism industry would largely rely on the good conduct of its tourist guides. It is of great significance to have all the tourist guides pass holders as well as future guides understood "dos and don'ts"; otherwise, misbehavior of tourist guides would not only ruin the reputation and future career of him/her, but also destroy the fragile tourist industry of China.

This chapter mainly looks at legal and ethical issues in tour guiding. It begins with a list of laws, regulations, rules and standards that guides should keep in mind. Nevertheless, they are also bound by the code of conduct and ethical obligations of tour guiding.

Key Words and Phrases

Interim /'ɪnt(ə)rɪm/ *noun*: a period of time between events :interval.

Procuring /prə'kjuə/ *verb*: to get (something) by some action or effort, obtain.

Liability /ˌlaɪə'bɪlɪti/ *noun*: the state of being legally responsible for something: the state of being liable for something.

Provision /prə'vɪʒ(ə)n/ *noun*: something that is done in advance to prepare for something else.

Compensation /ˌkɒmpen'seɪʃ(ə)n/ *noun*: something that is done or given to make up for damage, trouble, etc.

Prejudice /ˈpredʒudɪs/ *noun*: a feeling of like or dislike for someone or something especially when it is not reasonable or logical.

Propaganda /ˌprɒpəˈɡændə/ *noun*: usually disapproving, ideas or statements that are often false or exaggerated and that are spread in order to help a cause, a political leader, a government, etc.

Commission /kəˈmɪʃ(ə)n/ *noun*: an amount of money paid to an employee for selling something.

Solicit /səˈlɪsɪt/ *verb*: to ask (a person or group) for money, help, etc.

Integrity /ɪnˈteɡrɪti/ *noun*: the quality of being honest and fair.

Objectivity /ˌɒbdʒekˈtɪvɪti/ noun: the state or quality of being objective and fair.

Enthusiasm /ɪnˈθjuːziæz(ə)m/ *noun*: strong excitement about something, a strong feeling of active interest in something that you like or enjoy.

Sensitive /ˈsensɪtɪv/ *adjective*: having an understanding of something, aware of something.

Complimentary /ˌkɒmplɪˈmentəri/ *adjective*: given for free.

Review Questions

1. Please list the regulations guiding the behaviors of tourist guides.
2. Please list the regulations guiding the behaviors of travel companies.
3. Discuss code of guiding practice.
4. Discuss ethical obligations of guiding.

Choice Questions

Choose the best answer to the questions below. You need to correctly answer 3 of the 5 questions to pass.

1. Which of the following is not regarded as the fundamentals of being

ethical as a professional tourist guide in this book?

    A. To dress appropriately for the type of tour being conducted

    B. To have a wide range of knowledge

    C. To know and follow the policies of the company

    D. To solicit gratuities

2. Which of the following should not be conducted by professional tourist guide?

    A. To act honestly, fairly, professionally and reasonable in all dealings

    B. To regularly update and upgrade the guiding skills and knowledge

    C. To make use of fraudulent acts to collect commission

    D. To provide all goods and services as presented in the tour itinerary and promotional material

3. In adherence to the *Rules of Travel Agencies "Procuring Insurance of Travel Agencies" Liability by Order No.14 of the National Tourism Administration*, the fee limit of accidental death and disability benefit is?

    A. 200 thousand Yuan

    B. 300 thousand Yuan

    C. 400 thousand Yuan

    D. 500 thousand Yuan

4. According to the *Regulations on Management of Tourist Guide released by the CNTA*, what is the possible penalty if a tourist guide forget wearing on their chest the tourist Guide Pass and take inappropriate attitude to his/her ill-conduct, when performing his/her duty?

    A. 500 *Yuan*

    B. 1 000 *Yuan*

    C. 2 000 *Yuan*

    D. Nothing happens

5. A code of practice is not a law, but it should be followed unless there is an alternative course of action that achieves the same or better standards.

A. True

B. False

Group Discussion

Recently the Tour Guide ID card issued by European Tour Operators' Association (ETOA) to its members arouses hot debate in European counties.

ETOA argues that the main objective of the ID card scheme is to support the freedom of tourist guides working in Europe to deliver cultural commentary to tourists in public places without interference.

However, FEG, the official European representative body of 40 000 professional tourist guides across 21 countries expressed clear opposition to the practice of ETOA. FEG states that members of FEG have independently recognized ID (in/for the country, region or city they work) and have dealt directly with tens of millions of visitors. More importantly, there are already mechanisms within the EU that deal with cross-border services for all professions. ETOA, being the trade organization for a number of tour operators clearly recognizes that in reality it has no standing to issue an ID for a Profession and has trailed a scheme that is flawed. In general, this sort of idea from ETOA just muddies the waters, misinforms the market and consumers and could harm the image of tourism.

Source: www.feg-touristguides.com/.../205-feg-press-release-ref-etoa-id-card

1. Why does FEG strongly oppose the tour guide ID card issued by ETOA?

2. Will tourist guides in European countries support the Card issued by ETOA, or not?

Guiding Exercise

After every tourist gets into his or her room at Kempinski Hotel, Chengdu, you would like to discuss the itinerary with Mr. Colgan, a tour leader from American Express Travel.

Legal and Ethical Issues in Tour Guiding

According to the schedule, you are going to visit Chengdu Research Base of Giant Panda Breeding tomorrow morning. At noontime, you will have lunch at Gingko restaurant. In the afternoon, you are supposed to visit Chengdu Wuhou Shrine.

Please confirm this schedule with Mr. Colgan and further discuss if there is any adjustment to it.

Translation Exercise

1. Please translate the following passage into Chinese.

Tourist guides shall strive to provide visitors with the highest standard of service in accordance with the provisions of the travel service contract and the itinerary. The itinerary shall not be altered without the consent of the visitors and the travel agent concerned. If alteration is necessary because of emergencies or special circumstances, tourist guides shall seek approval from their travel agent and clearly explain the reasons for such alteration to the visitors.

2. Please translate the following passage into English.

导游不得以任何形式，向旅客收取或代为收取任何以中途离团、年龄、职业等为理由的额外费用，即使按内地组团社指示也不可以，但旅客因参加自费活动而需缴付的费用则除外。

Case Study

15名上海游客参加了某旅行社组织的马尔代夫7日游，每人交纳了10 980元团费。在马尔代夫的第三天行程中导游吴亮突然宣布：后三天的行程将增加自费旅游景点，安排"A、B套餐"，A套餐每人2 800元、B套餐每人1 500元。游客马上质疑：旅行社在出团行程中已经安排了后三天的参观活动，缘何还要增加自费项目并捆绑销售？最后经交涉，导游同意将B套餐中减去两项，每人交1 080元。

1. 本案中导游员吴亮的违规之处有哪些？应该受到怎样的处罚？
2. 应如何避免类似事件的发生，保护旅游者的合法权益？

Further Reading

Tourist Guides' Professional Ethics in Hongkong

Tourist guides shall strive to provide visitors with the highest standard of service in accordance with the provisions of the travel service contract and the itinerary. The itinerary shall not be altered without the consent of the visitors and the travel agent concerned. If alteration is necessary because of emergencies or special circumstances, tourist guides shall seek approval from their travel agent and clearly explain the reasons for such alteration to the visitors.

Tourist guides shall maintain a good and incorruptible working relationship with partners such as tour escorts and tour coach drivers, and the staff of all service providers such as attractions, hotels, restaurants and tour coach companies, to ensure that the services specified in contracts are provided at the highest level.

Tourist guides shall abide by, and help visitors to understand and abide by, the laws of Hong Kong.

Tourist guides shall adhere to professional ethics. When receiving visitors they shall: be dutiful, sincere, courteous and attentive; speak and act cautiously, discreetly, and be objective in their attitude; be knowledgeable about Hong Kong; provide visitors with accurate information; respect the religious belief, customs and habits of visitors; be punctual in performing duties; not smoke in front of visitors and drink alcohol during work; not gamble during work; not sell illicit items to visitors or recommend them to buy such items; and not seize or take away or attempt to seize or take away the travel documents of visitors unless such an act is made on proper grounds and lasts for a reasonable time.

Tourist guides shall dress properly to enhance their professional image. When performing their duties, they shall wear on their chest the Tourist Guide Pass issued by the TIC.

Tourist guides shall ensure sustained development of the industry.

Principles on the acceptance of gratuities:

- To maintain a professional image, tourist guides shall not collect gratuities by any coercive means, nor shall they exhibit dissatisfaction, provide sub-standard service or refuse to provide service because few or no gratuities are given.
- Tourist guides shall follow their travel agents' policies concerning gratuities and shall not make use of any fraudulent acts to collect them.

(Source: http://www.tichk.org/public/website/en/guides/code/html.)

Chapter 6

Job Description of Guiding Group

Learning Outcomes

After reading this chapter, you will be able to:

- Understand the job description of a tour manager, tour operator and tour leader, tour escort, local tour guide and on-site guide
- Be aware of the typical work of a tour manager, tour operator and tour leader, tour escort, local tour guide and on-site guide

Opening Case

A physical altercation occurred between a Hong Kong tour ist guide and mainland tourists in To Kwa Wan of Kowloon, Hong Kong, where 4 people suffered injuries were then sent to the hospital, and were subsequently detained at the Hong Kong Hong Hum police station for investigation. The tourists claim that they were taken to a jewelry store to shop, but because they did not buy anything, the tour guide used foul language to hurl abuse at them, thus resulting in the quarrel.

"I'll scold you if you refuse shopping!" screams "a certain tour guide" in "Hong Kong" at a "mainland tour group" while "a certain travel agency" holds a "zero base salary" knife to her back. The cartoon suggests that Hong Kong tourist guides may mistreat mainland tourists because they are forced by travel agencies to rely only on commissions earned when the tourists spend money shopping at the stores that the tour guides take them to.

(Source: http://www.chinasmack.com/2011/stories/hong-kong-tour-guide-curses- fights-with-mainland-tourists.html.)

1. What is your interpretation of the cartoon?
2. Please discuss how to prevent this incident.

Introduction

Within large tour company, employees work in a variety of functions, including marketing, IT, public relations, operations, sales and contracts, or resort representatives within hotels and resorts; smaller tour company employ few staff, who performs a wide range of duties, varying according to the time of year.

In this chapter, we will further clarify the job description as well as typical work activities that each member in the guiding group would have. We will mainly focus on members like travel agency manager, tour operator and tour leader, tourist guide and tour escort who are essential components in a successful tour company.

Job Description of Guiding Group

6.1 Tour Manager

Tour manager, also known as tour director, is responsible for managing an outlet for *retail* and/or business travel products, particularly for sales development, staff and financial management and day-to-day operational management. Managers need to be able to work in an increasingly competitive environment which includes offering online and fax booking services at reduced prices to busy customers.

Knowledge Links [6-1]

> 旅行社经理是指旅行社聘用的总经理（副总经理）和部门经理或同级业务主管人员。旅行社经理资格证书包括：国际旅行社总经理资格证书、国际旅行社部门经理资格证书、国内旅行社总经理资格证书、国内旅行社部门经理资格证书。
>
> 旅行社经理人员必须是中华人民共和国公民。其中，国际旅行社总经理（副总经理）应当具有大学专科以上学历，在旅行社部门经理岗位工作3年以上，或从事其他旅游经济管理工作5年以上。旅行社总经理（副总经理）资格考试科目为旅行社经营管理、政策与法规。旅行社部门经理或同级业务主管人员资格考试科目为：旅游经济（旅行社）专业知识与实务（初级）、政策与法规。
>
> （资料来源：旅行社经理资格认证管理规定.）

As travel agencies range from small independent organizations dealing with a wide range of customers, to specialist agencies that have in-depth knowledge of their product, to the large chains who offer everything to everyone, the job of a tour manager offers much scope for variety and *progression.*

As a manager, inevitably a typical week will involve:
- Dealing with staffing issues;
- Keeping the business running smoothly;
- Working closely with team leaders.

As this is a product-driven industry inspiring all staff to have the same levels of interest and *enthusiasm* for hitting sales, targets is also a big part of the role. Marketing and selling travel and holiday products involve:
- Constantly motivating the sales team to hit their targets and thus ensure profitability of the company;
- Meeting on a weekly basis with team leaders to give them sales figures and plan how they approach their work;
- Meeting regularly with company directors who advise on moving the company forward and finding out about any local issues;
- Overseeing the recruitment and selection of staff, payroll matters, and staff training;
- Occasional selling;
- Problem solving;
- Organizing incentives and competitions;
- Communicating with other branches and sometimes visiting them;
- Spending time talking to sales consultants on the sales floor and providing encouragement or offering help and advice to them.

6.2 Tour Operator

Tour operators or "OP" for short, create, arrange and operate tours and travel programmes, making contracts with *hoteliers*, airlines and ground transport companies. They market their tours either through travel agencies or directly to customers via websites, digital television and other advertising. They may also arrange for the printing and distribution of brochures advertising the holidays that they have assembled.

They are the organizers and providers of package holidays, unlike travel agents, who give advice, sell and administer bookings for tour operators. Around a thousand tour operators in China offer holiday tours, ranging from those providing over athousand holidays a year to the smaller specialist firms.

Knowledge Links [6-2]

> 旅游计调师又称为计调，是指在旅游企业里为团体或个人提供旅游计划采购及调度服务及其相关服务的专业人员。计调工作主要流程包括：①关注门票、住宿、用餐、用车、导游等动态价格情况；②接听业务电话，并做好记录；③核算成本，快速报价；④落实人数、用房数、特殊要求等；⑤签订合同，约定结账方式，并盖章确认；⑥安排团队的接待计划，做到五订(订房、订票、订车、订导游、订餐)；⑦催收团款；⑧做好跟踪服务；⑨资料归档。
>
> （资料来源：米学俭，尚永利，等. 旅游计调师操作标准教程. 2 版. [M]. 北京：旅游教育出版社，2012.）

The work activities involved will vary according to the size of the tour company:

- Planning which countries and resorts to use, and the number of holidays to offer, using information from previous seasons and market research;
- *Negotiating* with hoteliers, airlines, coach operators and venues to make provisional bookings at agreed costs;
- Making visits to resorts and *accommodation* to check its *suitability* and quality standards;
- Preparing *brochures* or websites, giving information about prices, arranging photographs and descriptions, in *compliance* with legislation;

- Organizing the launch of the brochure/website to individual clients and tour operators, with particular emphasis on any new initiatives;
- *Liaising* with airlines and hoteliers to ensure that they can continue to offer the level of agreed service;
- Handling bookings received, and forecasting number of holidays sold, making adjustments as necessary;
- Liaising with resort representatives, hoteliers, coach operators and airlines;
- Organizing the issuing of tickets to customers, and invoicing, either directly or via travel agents;
- Confirming names of customers to airlines, hotels and overseas staff;
- Reviewing the process continually, evaluating customer feedback, and taking action where necessary.

6.3 Tour Leader

Tour leader is the person who normally possesses a tour leader qualification issued and/or recognized by the appropriate authority, and travels with a group of holiday-makers on a package tour to a wide variety of locations overseas. As the representative of the travel company, they act as a guide and coordinate with tour escort and local tour guide from overseas company to ensure that the itinerary, facilities and services promised are provided.

Tour leader are responsible for accompanying and organizing the tour from beginning to end, whether it lasts a few days or several weeks. In some companies, before tours are publicized and booked by the public, tour leader work on planning and organization. Tour leader works for tour companies, which can be large, national or international companies or smaller, special interest operators.

Job Description of Guiding Group

Knowledge Links [6-3]

> "海外领队"是指接受具有经营出境旅游业务资格的旅行社委派、全权代表旅行社带领旅游团从事旅游活动的工作人员。他既是旅行社的代表，也是旅游团的领导和代言人。"领队业务"是指为出境旅游团提供旅途全程陪同和有关服务；作为组团社的代表，协同境外接待旅行社（简称"接待社"）完成旅游计划安排；以及协调处理旅游过程中相关事务等活动。领队人员应当履行下列职责：①遵守《中国公民出国旅游管理办法》中的有关规定，维护旅游者的合法权益以及人身和财物安全；②落实旅游合同，监督旅游计划的实施，协同接待社实施旅游行程计划，协助处理旅游行程中的突发事件、纠纷及其他问题；③介绍情况、全程陪同，为旅游者提供旅游行程服务；④自觉维护国家利益和民族尊严，并提醒旅游者抵制任何有损国家利益和民族尊严的言行；⑤其他工作，如组织、团结与联络工作。
>
> （资料来源：《出境旅游领队人员管理办法》.)

Typical works of tour leaders in China include:

- Abiding by the "Administrative Regulations Concerning Chinese People's Tours to Foreign Countries" to ensure the rights and benefits of tourists;
- Working together with tour escort and local tourist guide to liaison with hotels, coach companies, restaurants and other clients, and to assist handling emergencies and incidents;
- Safeguarding the national benefits and national dignity, and reminding tourists to avoid any improper behaviors or conducts;
- Visiting destinations, offering suggestions on interesting travel routes or places of interest and making accommodation bookings on proposed dates;
- Accompanying groups travelling by coach, although on specialist tours, travel may be by mini-bus, car, boat, train or plane;
- Welcoming groups of **holidaymakers** at their starting point, checking that all members of the group have arrived and, if not, making investigations through the company;

- Checking tickets and other relevant documents, seat allocations and any special requirements;
- *Commentating*, during the journey, on places of interest along the route;
- Informing passengers of arrival and departure times at each destination on the itinerary (including ensuring that all members of the group are back on the coach before departing from each stop);
- Providing information on places where the group stops for accommodation, meals or sightseeing;
- Ensuring that the tour is running smoothly for individual members of the group; answering any questions and offering help with any problems that arise. These can be as simple as directing a member of the group to the nearest chemist or arranging help with luggage, but could also include tracing property left behind at a hotel or restaurant, or helping a holidaymaker who is ill or needs to contact a family member urgently;
- Contacting places to stay or visit, ahead of arrival time, to check details and arrangements;
- *Utilizing* language skills for effective communication, during a tour and at the planning stages;
- Writing reports.

6.4 Tour Escort

Tour escort is appointed by domestic travel company, and coordinates with overseas tour leader and local tour guide or tour operator, who provides basic assistance to travelers and leads a group throughout a country or part of a country.

Job Description of Guiding Group

Knowledge Links [6-4]

> 全程陪同导游人员（以下简称全陪），指受国内组团旅行社委派，作为组团社的代表，在领队（由海外旅行社委派）和地方陪同导游人员的配合下实施接待计划，为旅游团（者）提供全程陪同服务的导游人员。其主要职责是：实施旅游计划；贯彻既定的接待方针和接待规格；做好上下站的联系工作；掌握全程活动的连贯性和一致性；妥善解决和处理途中的突发事件，遇有重大问题及时向有关部门汇报，听取意见和方法；做好工作日记，任务结束后做好善后事宜；联络工作，组织协调工作；维护安全、处理问题与事故；宣传、调研等。

Typical work activities include:

- Cooperating with tour leader and local tourist guide to liaison with hotels, coach companies, restaurants and other clients;
- Ensuring that the tour is running smoothly;
- Organizing the issuing of tickets and invoicing, either directly or via travel agents;
- Managing the tour group;
- Handling conflicts and emergencies on behalf of the tour operator;
- Promoting and researching.

6.5 Local Tour Guide

The person who points out and comments on the highlights of the city is called a city guide or local guide. When the local guide doubles the duty by driving the vehicle, that person becomes a driver-guide.

Knowledge Links [6-5]

> 地方陪同导游人员（以下简称地陪），指受接待旅行社委派，代表接待社实施旅游计划，为旅游团（者）提供当地旅游活动安排、讲解或翻译等服务的导游人员。其主要职责是安排旅游活动；做好接待工作；导游讲解和翻译。

Typical work activities include:

- Representing the area (site, city, region and/or country);
- Guiding groups or individual visitors (including those with special needs) around natural and man-made attractions of an area;
- Researching and developing information in order to provide accurate and relevant commentaries;
- Interpreting for visitors the cultural and natural heritage as well as the environment;
- Helping visitors to experience and understand what they are viewing and/or visiting;
- Informing visitors on all the relevant aspects of life in the area;
- Creating and/or developing guided tours in their area;
- Using appropriate language;
- *Assess* their audience;
- Adjusting to their respective interests and requirements by selecting relevant information;
- Presenting the appropriate information in a comprehensive and communicative way.

6.6 On-Site Guide

On-site guide is to provide the highest level of customer service, answer *enquiries* and to deliver a range of *informative* and *accurate* commentaries to visitors.

Knowledge Links [6-6]

> 景点景区导游人员（简称讲解员），指在某一旅游景区（景点）内，负责为旅游团（者）进行导游讲解服务的导游人员。其主要职责是安全提示和导游讲解。

Typical work activities include:
- Delivering exceptional customer service and presenting oral interpretation to visitors to the site as described in the Interpretation Plan and Guiding Department Standards;
- Participating in the improvement of the guiding business unit by attending training sessions;
- Providing relevant and accurate information to visitors regarding activities, features and facilities;
- Undertaking other relevant tasks and duties as directed by the guiding manager.

Summary

Summary

This chapter clarifies the job description as well as typical work activities of different kinds of tourist guides, namely, tour manager, tour operator and tour leader, local tour guide, tour escort and on-site tour guide.

It begins with the job description of tour manager, who manages an outlet for retail and/or business travel products, and is responsible for sales development, staff and financial management and day-to-day operational management. Then, it goes to introduce the tour operator whose responsibilities mainly involve creating, arranging and operating tours.

Comparing the job description of tour leader with tour escort, we would find out that they have similar typical work activities, which makes many learners easily get confused. The most obvious difference between the two is that tour leader would travel overseas, while tour escort would work within a country or a part of it. It is relatively easy to recognize the job of local tour guide, due to its popularity among the public, mostly involving guiding, interpreting, informing and communicating. The chapter is concluded with the job description of on-site guide whose daily work includes answering enquiries and delivering informative and accurate commentaries.

Key Words and Phrases

Retail /'riːˌteɪl/ *noun*: the business of selling things directly to customers for their own use.

Progression /prəˈgreʃ(ə)n/ *noun*: a continuous and connected series of actions, events, etc.

Hotelier /həʊˈteljə/ *noun*: a person who owns or operates a hotel.

Negotiate /nɪˈgəʊʃɪˌeɪt/ *verb*: to discuss something formally in order to make an agreement.

Accommodation /əkɒməˈdeɪʃ(ə)n/ *noun*: a place (such as a room in a hotel) where travelers can sleep and find other services.

Suitability /ˌsuːtəˈbɪlɪti/ *noun*: the degree to which something or someone has the right qualities for a particular purpose.

Brochure /ˈbrəʊʃə, brɒˈʃʊə/ *noun*: a small, thin book or magazine that usually has many pictures and information about a product, a place, etc.

Compliance /kəmˈplaɪəns/ *noun*: the act or process of doing what you have been asked or ordered to do, the act or process of complying.

Initiative /ɪˈnɪʃətɪv/ *noun*: the power or opportunity to do something before others do.

Liaise /lɪˈeɪz/ *verb*: to make it possible for two organizations or groups to work together and provide information to each other : to act as a liaison — usually + with or between.

Publicize /ˈpʌblɪˌsaɪz/ *verb*: to cause (something) to be publicly known, to give information about (something) to the public.

Holidaymaker /ˈhɒlɪdeɪˌmeɪkə/ *noun*: a person who is on holiday away from where they usually live.

Commentate /ˈkɒmənˌteɪt/ *verb*: to provide a description on a radio or television program of an event (such as a sports contest) as it is happening.

Utilize /ˈjuːtiˌlaiz/ *verb*: to use (something) for a particular purpose.

Assess /əˈses/ *verb*: to make a judgment about (something).

Enquiry /inˈkwaiəri/ *noun*: the act of asking for information.

Informative /inˈfɔːmətiv/ *adjective*: providing useful knowledge or ideas.

Accurate /ˈækjurət/ *adjective*: correct and without any mistakes.

Review Questions

1. Please discuss the job description of tour manager, tour operator and tour leader, local tour guide, tour escort and on-site tour guide.

2. Please compare the typical work activities of tour leader with that of tour escort.

Choice Questions

Choose the best answer to the questions below. You need to correctly answer 3 of the 5 questions to pass.

1. The typical work activities of the on-site guide may not include?

A. Delivering exceptional customer service and present oral interpretation to visitors to the site as described in the Interpretation Plan and Guiding Department Standards

B. Participating in the improvement of the guiding business unit by attending training sessions

C. Cooperating with tour leader and local tour guide to liaison with hotels, coach companies, restaurants and other clients

D. Undertaking other relevant tasks and duties as directed by the guiding manager

2. The typical work activities of local tourist guide may exclude?

A. Helping visitors to experience and understand what they are viewing and/or visiting

B. Preparing brochures or websites, giving information about prices

C. Guiding groups or individual visitors around natural and man-made attractions of an area

D. Informing visitors on all the relevant aspects of life in the area

3. Tour leader is the person who normally possesses a tour leader qualification issued and/or recognized by the appropriate authority, and travels with a group of holiday-makers on a package tour to a wide variety of locations overseas?

A. True

B. False

4. Tour escort is appointed by domestic travel company, and coordinates with overseas tour leader and local tour guide or tour operator, who provides basic assistance to travelers and leads a group throughout a country or part of a country?

A. True

B. False

5. Tour manager, creates, arranges and operates tours and travel programmes, making contracts with hoteliers, airlines and ground transport companies.

A. True

B. False

Group Discussion

The package tour market is an extremely competitive market with razor-thin profit margins for many travel agencies in China, and some agencies prefer to use unqualified guides who accept no or low salaries and for which there is an ample supply. Tour guides may sometimes even pay to bid for tour groups from tour operators. This obviously imposes the risk of the tour group being taken for more shopping excursions where the tour guide then gets a part of the sales commissions.

(Source: Leo Huang, Peng-Hsiang Kao. How to tell a good tour guide under different strategic orientations. African Journal of Business Management. 2011, Vol.5 (27).

1. Discuss the risk of employing unqualified guides.
2. Discuss what motives tourist guides to pay to bid for tour groups.

Guiding Exercise

At noontime, you are taking a group of tourists from US to have lunch at Gingko Restaurant in Chengdu. As informed earlier by the tour leader, in your group, there are several tourists who have special needs: Mr. Anderson, a vegetarian, who chooses not to eat meat; Ms. Green, a Muslim, who wants to taste chop steaks; Mr. Cooks are not so skillful at using chopsticks, who asks for knife and folk.

You are supposed to liaison with Miss Yu, the manager of the restaurant to meet their needs and wants.

Translation Exercise

1. Please translate the following passages into Chinese.

Standing southwest of Emeishan City, Sichuan province, Mt. Emei, an elevation of 3 099m, has been reputed as "the most elegant under heaven". Said to be the site of Bodhisattva of Universal Benevolence to expound the texts of Buddhism, the place saw Buddhism flourishing with each passing day in the period of Tang and Song, with Buddhist monasteries covering almost every mountain here.

There are over a hundred Buddhist niches and 40 caves, and moreover there are Wannian (Myriad Years) Temple, Baoguo (Serving the Country Worthily) Temple, Hongchun Plateau Qianfo (Thousand Buddha) Buddhist Monastery,

Elephant Washing Pond, Gold Summit Huacang (Lotus Flower Sutra) Temple and other historic interest sites.

2. Please translate the following passage into English.

乐山大佛，又名凌云大佛，地处中国四川省乐山市，位于岷江、青衣江和大渡河三江汇流处，与乐山城隔江相望。乐山大佛雕凿在岷江、青衣江和大渡河汇流处岩壁上，依岷江南岸凌云山栖霞峰临江峭壁凿造而成为弥勒佛坐像，是唐代摩崖造像的艺术精品之一，是世界上最大的石刻弥勒佛坐像，国家 5A 级旅游景区。

Case Study

澳大利亚某旅游团 10 日早上到达云南丽江，按计划上午参观玉龙雪山，下午自由活动，晚上 20:00 观看《印象·丽江》演出。抵达当天，适逢当地举行通宵篝火歌舞晚会等丰富多彩的文艺节目。Mr.Cogan 等三位团友提出，下午想去参加篝火晚会，放弃观看晚上的文艺演出。导游员邱某提出全团必须一起活动，要求所有的团友都观看《印象·丽江》演出。Mr.Cogan 等游客迫于导游员强硬的态度，只能无奈同意。但在回到澳大利亚后，这些游客将导游员邱某投诉到了当地旅游主管部门。

1. 邱某应受到怎样的处罚？
2. 针对案例中的情况，导游人员应该怎样处理？应做好哪些工作？

Further Reading

European Federation of Tourist Guide Associations

FEG was founded in 1986 in Paris to represent the profession at European level, to publicise and improve the quality of service offered to all visitors to Europe and to bring together and strengthen professional tourist guiding links across Europe.

22 years later in 2008, FEG is the voice of professional tourist guides in the

Europe and is recognized as an advocate of high standards and quality in tourism. It is an active member of the European Tourism Action Group (ETAG) and a participant or observer in key European forums.

FEG gives professional tourist guides a voice in Europe. Over 20 years FEG has been able to achieve a much higher profile for tourist guides in Europe and has itself become recognized and respected as a relevant lobby for its profession. In fact it is increasingly the case that European organizations prefer to consult with other European organizations rather than with local or national groups. As a result FEG representatives attend and/or sit on a number of pan-European groupings and FEG contributes on a regular basis to discussions on all aspects of the tourism industry in Europe. FEG was a member of the Commission's Sustainable Tourism Group, which reported in March 2007 and in 2009, will be contributing to the new Social Tourism Working Party.

Historically tourist Guiding has developed for decades as a distinct profession within the tourism industry alongside other complimentary professions that also contribute to the visitors' overall experience. Professional qualifications for tourist guides in European countries have helped raise quality and standards and in a number they are needed to practice the profession.

FEG, at its meeting in Prague in February 2006, finalized its own document, 'Tourist Guide Training — The Way Forward'. As a consensus of views of its Members the Document establishes common criteria for tourist guide training and identifies common subjects for modules. It additionally emphasizes the importance of language skills and compliments FEG's documents on language testing. Crucially it recognizes that the vocation of tourist guiding comprises the interaction of knowledge and practical skills and sets out how this can delivered in training. FEG's wealth of experience, its involvement in so many countries and its members' unique position in so often being the link between destinations and the visitor makes this a 'best practice' document of help to training providers across Europe.

Job Description of Guiding Group

As the EU expands over the next few years there will naturally be much greater cross-border supply of services and the issue of equivalence of professional qualifications from one country to another will grow in importance. FEG is well aware of this and recognizes that a vital part of its work is to consider the issue in relation to tourist guiding. Whether tourist guiding is regulated in a country or not it will become increasingly important to be able to establish how one country's training and qualification relates to another.

A further way in which FEG and its members have helped to promote an understanding of what professional tourist guides do has been the development of a quality charter. By pooling resources, a FEG quality charter was approved by all its Members. It will help clients understand exactly what they could expect of tourist guides all over Europe. The quality charter has been adopted by the WFTGA.

There is yet another side to FEG, outside the EU work and representing Tourist Guides in Europe. It is the role FEG can play in bringing the various and often disparate tourist guide associations together for mutual benefit. Often this might be to share common challenges or to share information – issues such as site liaison, new European legislation and regulations (e.g. in relation to coaches, requests to know the services provided by colleagues across Europe, which markets are growing or shrinking etc.).

(Source: www.feg-touristguides.org.)

Chapter 7
Essential Steps for Guiding

Learning Outcome

After reading this chapter, you will be able to:

- Understand seven essential steps in tour guiding
- Be aware of what should be well prepared in the pre-tour arrangement
- Know how to meet group at airport, bus station or train station
- Learn how to deliver a welcome speech and farewell speech
- Describe the procedures of checking-in and checking-out
- Recognize that there are many other services like shopping, meeting, etc.
- Realize the work activities after seeing tourists off

Opening Case

Several local tourist guides gathered last night (2/15/2011) outside a hotel-casino protesting against a group of mainland tourists who had earlier attacked a local tourist guide, demanding that they apologize.

According to some observers, there were as many as 100 tourist guides in the area surrounding Jai Alai casino. Eventually, the guides surrounded the group's coach to demand an apology for the attack. The police and the Macau Government Tourist Office deputy director rushed to the scene to maintain order and calm. The confrontation lasted for five hours. As no agreement was reached, the police drove the tourists back to their hotel in police vehicles.

Earlier in the morning, a group of 26 Liaoning province tourists complained about their tourist guide, accusing him of being late and of not holding any information board for them to recognize him by. Actually, the group had arrived ahead of schedule at the ferry terminal, according to the Tourist Office. A tourist guide from a different travel agency tried to mediate the conflict at the ferry terminal, but 3 members of the group allegedly attacked him. He received some minor injuries and rushed to the hospital. The police have identified the alleged aggressors.

(Source: http://www.macaubusiness.com/news/conflict-arises-between-local-tour-guides-and-group-of-mainland-tourists/7557/.)

1. What is your comment on the above incident?
2. Discuss both the negative and positive effect of the conflicts.

Introduction

It is widely accepted that "work procedure is the guarantee for service qualities". Therefore, guiding techniques, above all, are manifested as some 7 essential steps. In this chapter, we are going to discuss them one after another.

Before we start to go, there is one thing for you to know, that is, as discussed in chapter 6, there are similarities paired with differences as respect to the job descriptions for escort, tourist guide or tour leader. Regarding this fact, it seems that there is no need to spend time to touch the working procedure for each one of them here; however, if you like, we will mainly focus on how local tourist guide do his or her job. All right, let begin.

Essential Steps for Guiding

7.1 Pre-Tour Arrangement

7.1.1 Good Understanding of the Task

The first thing goes first. Therefore, the first step is to have a good understanding of the task (or what to do), before you actually decide to take it. If you think that the job is really the one you would like to have after having a nice talk with tour operator or tour manager, it is strongly suggested to check out the following information at the so-called "pre-tour stage". If you have any question about the following details, it is your privilege as well as duty to ask the one concerned. That is to make sure that there will not be any errors or regrets incurred by misunderstanding (Figure 7.1).

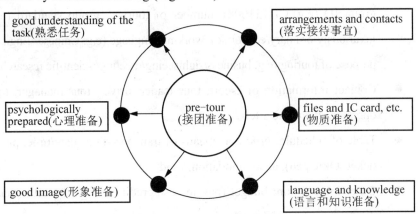

Figure 7.1 pre-tour arrangements

Knowledge Links [7-1]

> 导游员工作任务单或委派单是旅行社委派导游员执行带团任务的凭据，由委派带团任务的旅行社开具。借调单由导游服务公司或者导游证挂靠单位开具并加盖公章后，再交由委派旅行社确认并加盖公章。运行计划表由委派旅行社的计调人员填写并加盖公章，应详细写明该团的详细行程、餐、房、车等信息，它是导游人员执行旅游接待任务的依据。行程单由委派旅行社的计调人员填写并加盖公章，用于简要地说明用餐、住宿、游览等行程安排，供导游与游客及领队人员交流行程安排所用。以上文件的正式文本均为一式两份(行程单复印件供游客留存)，旅行社及导游员各一份。导游人员担任导游任务时，必须携带接待计划书及行程安排单，如果是临时借调的导游人员，还需要携带借调单。由于在运行计划表中注明了导游的带团任务等信息，故部分旅行社省略了开具委派单的环节。

The information a tourist guide should prepare is listed below:

- ***Demographical*** information of tourists: name, gender, age, occupation, education background, salary, religious belief, nationality.
- Basic information about tour group: group title (e.g. "Happy Trip"), group ID (e.g. CHT11008), number of tourists, group standard (e.g. luxuriously/ordinary/economic), working language (e.g. Chinese/ English), purpose of touring (e.g. business/sightseeing/meeting/ scientific research).
- Contact information of escort, tour leader, driver, tour manager, tour operator, just name a few.
- Table of schedule: *itinerary*, means of transportation (date/time, place, ticket: Ok/Open), accommodation, food.
- Other information: budget (pay in cash/credit, or sign the bill), ticket discount, and special needs.

7.1.2 Contacts and Arrangements

If you got the guiding task a few days earlier than it is supposed to start, it is a safe way to contact with those in your working team before it really goes. Because, anything could happen for various excuses, probably, the trip might be delayed, changed or even canceled. In case of having no idea about what to do next, it is better to keep the information about the schedule updated as time goes close to the start point.

- As a tourist guide, you should contact with tour operator and many other staff members in your working group, and make some arrangements 1 or 2 days before the arrival of the tourists.
- To contact with tour operator to ensure the arriving date, and to find out if there are any adjustments or changes (e.g. number of tourists).
- To contact with driver and confirm with him/her the bus arrangement (e.g. date, bus/car, luggage *delivery* service).
- To contact with the hotel, restaurant, scenic spots to make reservation or book the ticket if it is needed.

7.1.3 Preparation Work

You are not a tourist but you are going to travel with them. That is to say that you will not only need to get those files and documents prepared as ordinary tourists do, but also have to get some specific staff ready as you are the one serving the tour.

- Files and documents: passport, ID card, visas, tourist guide's ID card.
- Paper work of the travel agency: itinerary (Appendix III), schedule (Appendix IV), name list (Appendix V), questionnaire for guiding service (Appendix VI), tickets, insurance file (Appendix VII) and receipt.
- Personal necessities: clothes, medicine, camera, book.
- Working staff: flag, map, mobile phone, louder-speaker, glasses, notebook, and sun-cream.

Knowledge Links [7-2]

出团前做好如下准备：①必备物品，如导游证件、身份证、护照(出境团)、游客名单、保险单、接团任务书、委派单、运行计划表、游客意见调查表、借调单、行程、预借团款及拨款清单（结算单）、社旗、社徽、导游话筒、接站牌、记事本、计算器及必要的小礼品等；②个人物品，如药品、相机、电话、墨镜、防晒霜、换洗衣物和盥洗物品等。

7.1.4 Language and Knowledge

As Rome was not built in a day, it is the same true as to the fact that you cannot have yourself turned to be an all round professional tourist guide. So, it is not difficult to understand that it takes efforts and pains to be knowledgeable and proficient in the chosen working language. As the saying goes, better late than never. If you remember this, it would help somehow even you start to prepare for them at the last moment.

- Knowledge about the place to visit: history, *folklore*, landscape, geography, population, economy, transportation, etc.
- Interesting topics.
- *Commentary*.
- Language: *idiom*, term, etc.

7.1.5 Personal Appearance

It is very important to remember that good image and proper *courtesy* shows who you are and whom you are representing.

It is interesting to ask tourists what a guide looks like in their eyes. The answer may be varied. One thing for sure is that clothes are very important to your image. We do not have uniforms, so we can not assume what suites you best as your personality may be very distinctive; however we ask you to be conscious of what you wear while interacting with your clients. As logic may dictate, you should know what to wear as a tourist guide if you are trying to be as professional as you should be.

Basically you should wear clothing that is comfortable; also make sure you wear comfortable shoes which will help you a lot when walking long distances, particularly in mountainous regions.

We would kindly remind you, please be conscious of your choice of clothing on the days you give a tour. Please don't wear as much apparel as you wish; please don't wear offensive T-shirts, ripped clothing, or clothing with negative messages. If you want to be a great guide, dress appropriately for the occasion.

- City guiding: tailored trousers or skirt for ladies with a jacket, tailored trousers for men with jacket.
- Country or island guiding: as for city but jackets may be replaced by smart sweaters; weatherproof clothing and footwear, depending on season.
- Outdoor activities: appropriate protective clothing for weather and conditions.
- Be aware of personal hygiene and condition of clothing.

7.1.6 Psychologically Prepared

Tour operator or tour manager will give you necessary support, but they are not supposed to be there on the site to replace you to serve or to do the guiding job. Undoubtedly, it is the tourist guide who will take care of the clients and make sure they will have a nice trip here and safe trip home.

With that respect, you should be stronger than you thought you are, both physically and psychically. At first place, be ready to overcome difficulties and solve problems; be happy to serve; and be calm when faced with complaints.

7.2 Meeting the Group

7.2.1 Final Confirmation and Arrangement

Before meeting the group, it is advisable for you as a tourist guide to confirm the arrival time of the group, as is not unusual to find out flights, trains or buses delayed or even canceled. When the above information is firmly confirmed via telephone, fax or email, you will need to pass that to the driver since he or she needs to go with you to pick up tourists at the scheduled time.

It is suggested that tourist guide gets to the airport or bus station about 30 minutes earlier than the arrival of tourists and it is better to arrive at the airport 1 hour earlier if tourists take international flight.

Please check frequently with the arrival information on the screen. Once it is confirmed, you are supposed to hold a welcome board together with flag to wait outside the arriving gate for them (Figure 7.2).

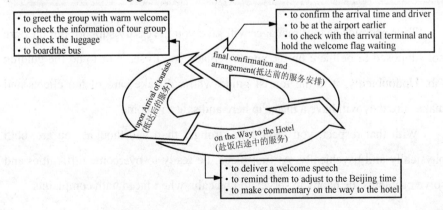

Figure 7.2 Meeting the group

Essential Steps for Guiding

Knowledge Links [7-3]

> 　　地陪导游员应与食宿、交通、游览等有关部门落实、核查旅游团（者）的交通、食宿、行李运输等事宜；确认旅游团（者）所乘交通工具及其准确抵达时间；与司机确认车辆停放的位置，需要时，在旅游团出站前与行李员取得联络，落实行李运输事宜。

7.2.2 Greetings and Boarding

After anxiously waiting for hours, you finally meet your guests with heavy luggage travelling long distance if everything goes on well. At this moment, please remember to greet the group with warm welcome, which is the first step to establish a welcoming rapport with them.

- Smile and greet the group with the appropriate greeting.
- Introduce yourself and the driver.
- Make a welcoming statement which is relevant to the group and the situation e.g., "Welcome to China, I hope you had a good journey".
- *Outline* the tour and inform the group of arrangements for breaks and likely arrival times.
- Inform them about heating and *ventilation* arrangements on the coach.
- Check numbers in the group.
- Check names if appropriate.
- Check if anyone has any questions.

Knowledge Links [7-4]

> 　　旅游团（者）出站后，地陪导游员应确认应接的旅游团，有全陪的，及时与全陪接洽；及时引导旅游团（者）前往停车场，在车门旁恭候旅游者上车，并协助旅游者就座；开车前礼貌地清点人数，以确保不落下旅游者；协助旅游者与全陪核对行李件数无误后将行李移交给行李员。

Knowledge Links [7-5]

> 游客集合等车之后，导游员应清点人数，并确保每位游客均已登车。清点人数时禁止用手指指着游客数数，一般以目光来点数，同时手垂下或放在身后，依照点数顺序弯曲手指。对于人数多的旅游团，可以由旅游车的座位数减去游客数得到相应的空座位数，这样每次确认空座位数无误即可。在清点人数完毕之后，应请全陪、领队或者较为积极的"团友"帮助确认没有落下任何一位游客，同时可建议每位游客选定固定座位，每次登车后请游客相互确认邻座的团友均已登车，若发现游客走失，应根据情况马上采取应急措施。

When meeting the group, you should also check the following information: group ID, name of the escort, tour leader, number of clients, etc. Please report all these to the tour operator as soon as possible, particularly when there is any adjustment to the itinerary or changes to number of guests. You should help the escort and tour leader check the luggage. When boarding the bus, you need to make sure everyone is there.

Knowledge Links [7-6]

> "错接"是指导游员接了不应该由他接的旅游团(者)的情况，也就是"张冠李戴"接错了团（人）；"漏接"是指旅游团抵达时没有导游人员迎接的情况。"空接"是指导游员按照指定时间到达之后发现旅游团被别人接走或者没有到达的情况。
>
> 导游员应认真研究运行计划表，仔细核对团号等基本信息，提前赶到接站地点，以避免漏接、错接和空接事故的发生。处理上述事故的基本原则：①立即汇报派团的旅行社；②联系相关人员，查明事故原因；③采取应急补救措施。

7.2.3 On the Way to the Hotel

When the engineer of the bus starts to power, you may announce, "Your journey to excellence begins here." After that, an experienced tourist guide may kindly remind his or her guests to sit back and relax while the bus is just leaving the airport or train station.

After a long journey from another city or country, most of your guests will be exhausted or tired, while some of them may feel really excited about the trip. It is not a wise choice to deliver a long speech. To be a non-stop talker will leave everyone of them a very bad first impression. By contrast, if you choose to speak what you are expected to say, that will be just perfect. They may be very much concerned about the following questions, such as who you are; where you are heading to; how long it takes to arrive there.

Generally speaking, when everyone feels comfortable on bus, you may begin your welcome speech. You would better make good use of the time on the way to the hotel or next destination by mentioning the key information while also extending warm welcome to them all. Basically, the following points are advised to be included.

- To extend a warm welcome;
- To introduce yourself as well as your working team;
- To remind them any safety issue or to adjust to the Beijing time;
- To make a brief commentary of the best of the city or the place to visit on the way to the hotel.

7.3 Checking-in the Hotel

Please remember that it is tour leader or escort who is often responsible for collecting the passport or ID card to complete the check-in *formality*. Moreover it is also the role of the above two persons to distribute room key/card to the guests, instead of local tourist guide. But, for small group or individual tourist, the check-in formality needs to be taken care by the local tourist guide. Usually a proportion of money is paid as *deposit* for room fee (Figure 7.3).

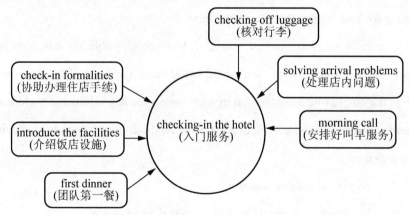

Figure 7.3 Checking-in the hotel

Knowledge Links [7-7]

全陪应做好分房方案并按照方案办妥入住登记手续。属于单位集体包团或入境游团队中有境外旅行社代表的,分房方案应分别交由包团单位代表或境外旅行社代表制定。

Essential Steps for Guiding

> 地陪导游员应及时办妥住店手续，热情引导旅游者进入房间和认找自己的大件交运行李，并进行客房巡视，处理旅游团(旅游者)入住过程中可能出现的各种问题。导游员还应该与饭店保持有效沟通和联系，落实住宿安排，取得客房钥匙，并告知旅游者如下信息：饭店基本设施和住店注意事项；饭店名称、位置和入店手续，有关服务项目和收费标准；当天或次日游览活动的安排，以及集合的时间、地点；饭店内就餐形式、地点、时间；全陪和旅游者的房间号，便于联系，导游员应等待行李送达饭店，核对行李，督促行李员及时将行李送至旅游者房间，以及安排次日的叫早服务。

Do not forget to set morning call with the help of the receptionist.

In the meantime, the **bellboy** is *offloading* and checking off luggage. In addition, what you need to do is to see to it that the bellboy has delivered the luggage to the right room.

You should briefly introduce the hotel facilities (e.g. room, restaurant, elevator, exchange) and location.

When the check-in formality is completed, clients may want to rest for a while in their room. Please remind them of the dinner time (if dinner is included), and then go to the restaurant to order the dish for them. You should circulate among them and see to their needs when they are having dinner.

You should try to solve problems that your clients have when *residing* in the hotel. The most common problems are:

- An occupied room;
- An inoperative television, air-conditioner;
- Less-than-enough beds in the room;
- No towels, or tooth paste;
- Unsatisfactory room;
- Untidy room.

7.4 Conducting the Tour

7.4.1 Gathering in the Lobby

It is suggested to follow the tips of proper behaviors below:
- **Be on time**: to get to the lobby 10~20 minutes before the departure time, and contact the driver; to make sure that everyone is showing up. If there is someone absent, make proper arrangement for him/her; to remind everyone to take his/her belongings with him/her.
- **Be yourself and be enthusiastic**: it is important that you offer your own personal experiences at the trip. These personal touches will make your tour more interesting and more memorable for tourists.
- **Know the facts**: in your role you are representing the local tourism industry and you have a responsibility to present accurate information to tourists.
- **Be flexible**: tourists often travel a great distance to visit, so your adaptability to different types of weather, sizes of groups, and energy level of tourists is crucial.
- **Encourage interactions with tourists**: be attentive to tourists when they ask questions and encourage participation. By doing this you will give a clear image of addressing of the group. Try to avoid wearing sunglasses.
- **Help all tourists feel welcome**: helping the local tourism come alive requires that all tourists feel comfortable during their entire visit. Your

language should send messages of value and respect for the diversity of people with whom you interact.
- **Be prepared:** know your goals for the tour and what images you are trying to convey.
- **It's okay to say, "I don't know":** it is far better to refer the tourist to a manager of the scenic area than to make up an answer or have a wide guess.

7.4.2 Travelling to the Destination

- To check again that everyone is boarding on the bus and say hello to them all.
- To make a brief commentary on the way to the destination.
- To sing a song or organize some interactive game with tourists.

Knowledge Links [7-8]

地陪导游员应提前到达集合地点，并督促司机做好出发前的各项准备工作。团队出发及每次移动前清点人数；前往景点的途中，向旅游团(者)介绍本地的风土人情、自然和人文景观，回答旅游者提出的问题，主动与旅游者进行交流；抵达景点前，向旅游者介绍该景点的简要情况，尤其是景点的背景、价值和特色；抵达景点时，告知旅游者在景点停留的时间，以及参观游览结束后集合的时间、地点及游览过程中的注意事项。

7.4.3 Delivering Commentary at the Scenic Spots

As is known to all, a group tour features that a tourist guide who travels with the group throughout the trip will provide sightseeing commentary and coordinate all group movement and activities. To be more specific, you are supposed to:

- Offer fixed route tours on foot in a specified site, or exceptionally on a moving vehicle like a boat or open-top bus;

- Have an in-depth knowledge of your site;
- Have a range of communication skills essential for the delivery of an effective commentary and presentation.

We will discuss more about a range of interpretation and presentation techniques designed to enhance the visitors experience in the following chapters.

Knowledge Links [7-9]

> 在游览过程中，尽量使用生动、风趣、吐字清晰易懂，富有感染力的讲解语言，对景点进行繁简适度的讲解，包括该景点的历史背景、特色、地位、价值等内容，使旅游者对景点的特色、价值、风貌、背景等及旅游者感兴趣的其他问题有基本的了解。当日游览活动结束时，了解旅游者对当日活动安排的反映并预报次日的活动日程、出发时间及其他有关事项。

7.5 Other Services

As discussed above, tourist guides have various roles to play in ensuring tourists a nice journey. It is not a surprise to find out that a tourist guide is also supposed to be an escort, an interpreter or a companion when tourists are doing shopping, having meeting, enjoying the opera or having dinner.

Those activities may or may not be included in the itinerary. Upon the request of tourists, you may add the so-called self-pay activities to the schedule. But any adjustment to the schedule should be agreed by your travel agent. More importantly, there are some rules for you to remember if you guide a group of tourists to take participate in the self-pay activities.

- Tourist guides shall only arrange self-pay activities for visitors which are approved by their travel agent.
- Tourist guides shall not compel visitors to join self-pay activities (including by such means as exerting group pressure or leaving visitors with no other choice), and shall allow visitors to choose freely whether to join such activities or not.
- Prior to arranging any self-pay activities, tourist guides shall explain clearly to visitors the content, fees, safety and responsibility issues.
- Tourist guides shall make appropriate arrangements according to the instructions of their travel agent for those visitors who choose not to join self-pay activities.

There are principles governing shopping activities for you to know.

- Tourist guides shall ensure that visitors understand their consumer rights, including: the right to make or not to make purchases; the right to obtain information on products and services; the freedom to choose products and services; and the right to complain, request their purchases to be exchanged or refunded.
- Tourist guides shall only arrange visits to those registered shops which are designated by their travel agent.
- Tourist guides shall not in any way compel or attempt to compel visitors to make purchases, or mislead or attempt to mislead them into doing so.
- Tourist guides shall allow visitors to freely leave or enter registered shops, and shall not force them to remain inside the shops.
- Tourist guides shall not allow their service attitude to be affected nor shall they refuse to perform their duties because of visitors' unwillingness to purchase or the value of their purchases.

7.6 Seeing the Group Off

7.6.1 Checking-out

- To get to the lobby 30 minutes before the departure time, and contact with the driver;
- To inform tourists the departure time;
- To remind tourists taking all their belongings;
- To get all the room cards from tour leader or tour escort (if there is one);
- To complete all the checking out formalities.

Knowledge Links [7-10]

> 离开酒店当天，地陪导游员应做好以下工作：集中交运行李；办理退房手续，并协助饭店结清与旅游者的有关账目；提醒旅游者带好身份证件及贵重物品；清点人数并集合登车。团队送行前，应提前确认或落实联程/返程交通票据，以确保团队能按时起程；商定并宣布行前集中行李、叫早、早餐及集合出发的时间；宣布有关离站的注意事项。

7.6.2 Travelling to Airport/Bus Station/Train Station/Port

- To check again that everyone is boarding on the bus and say hello to them all;

- To check the departure time of airport/bus station/train station/port;
- To make a *farewell* speech on the way to the destination;
- To organize some interactive games with tourists.

Knowledge Links [7-11]

> 离站送客时，地陪应代表各自的旅行社向旅游者致欢送词，向旅游者派发游客意见表，征询旅游者对旅游接待服务的意见；带领团队及时抵达机场（车站、码头）；办妥航班登机手续，向全陪移交机票及登机牌，并引导旅游团（者）依次通过机场安检；提醒旅游者保管好自己的物品和证件；引导旅游团（者）在候机楼或候车室休息等候，并按机场/车站的安排按时组织登机/车。

7.7 After Service Settlement

- To write a report to review and summarize the whole trip;
- To get to the accounting department/office of the travel company to settle the expense account (Appendix Ⅷ);
- To submit the service questionnaire.

Knowledge Links [7-12]

> 接团任务完成后导游员应填写并向旅行社递交导游日志，详细报告接团遇到的突发事件；尽快结清有关账目；做好带团总结。

Summary

Summary

The 7 essential steps of tour guiding are the fundamental techniques for ensuring quality services to the customers. Therefore, to have a clear understanding of each step is a task with great significance for learners to do.

As discussed, guiding service begins at pre-tour stage, which requires tourist guides to have a good understanding of the task and also get physically and psychologically prepared before the trip actually starts. Before meeting the group, it is suggested to make final confirmation and arrangement, and get to the airport or bus station earlier than the arrival time of the tourists. When meeting the group, tourist guide should greet the group with warm welcome. On the way to the hotel, tourist guide needs to delivery welcome speech and make a brief commentary. Upon arriving at the hotel, tourist guides are supposed to coordinate with tour leader, tour escort and receptionist to help completing the check-in formalities. Though conducting the tour is obviously the major task, we will leave space to discuss it further in the following chapters. Additionally, tourist guide is also expected to offer some other services in additional to thoseabove. After seeing the group off, the guiding service ends up with after service settlement.

Key Words and Phrases

Demographic /ˌdɪˈmɒgrəfɪk/ *adjective*: of or relating to the study of changes that occur in large groups of people over a period of time; of or relating to demography.

Itinerary /aɪˈtɪnəˌrəri/ *noun*: the places you go to or plan to go to on a journey, also a document in which the places you will be going to are listed.

Delivery /di'livəːri/ *noun*: the act of taking something to a person or place.

Folklore /'fəukˌlɔː/ *noun*: traditional customs, beliefs, stories, and sayings.

Commentary /'kɒmənˌt(ə)ri/ *noun*: spoken or written discussion in which people express opinions about someone or something.

Idiom /'idiəm/ *noun*: a form of a language that is spoken in a particular area and that uses some of its own words, grammar, and pronunciations.

Courtesy /'kəːtisi/ *noun*: polite behavior that shows respect for other people.

Outline /'aʊtˌlain/ *verb*: to list or describe only the most important parts of (an essay, speech, plan, etc.); to give an outline of (something).

Ventilate /'ventileit/ *verb*: to allow fresh air to enter and move through (a room, building, etc.).

Formality /fɔː'mæliti/ *noun*: something that is required or usual but that has little true meaning or importance.

Deposit /di'pɔːzit/ *noun*: money that you give someone when you agree to buy something (such as a house or car).

Bellboy /'belˌbɔi/ *noun*: a young man who carries bags, takes messages etc in a hotel.

Offload /ˌɔf'ləud/ *verb*: to remove (something) from a truck, ship, etc.

Reside /ri'zaid/ *verb*: to live in a particular place.

Farewell /feə'wel/ *adjective*: done when someone is leaving, ending a career, etc.

Review Questions

1. How many steps are there for tour guiding?
2. What should be well prepared in the pre-tour arrangement?
3. Discuss how to meet group at airport, bus station or train station.
4. How to deliver a welcome speech and farewell speech?
5. Describe the procedures of checking-in and check-out.
6. What are those work activities after seeing tourist off?

Choice Questions

Choose the best answer to the questions below. You need to correctly answer 3 of the 5 questions to pass.

1. It is strongly suggested to check out the following information at the "pre-tour stage", except:

    A. Contact information

    B. Table of schedule

    C. Demographical information of tourists

    D. Questionnaire for guiding service

2. How many minutes earlier than the arrival of tourists should tourist guide get to the airport?

    A. 30 minutes

    B. 60 minutes

    C. 40 minutes

    D. 50 minutes

3. Which is not regarded as the paper work of the travel agency that you should get prepared?

    A. Itinerary

    B. Schedule

    C. Insurance file

    D. Tourist guide's ID card

4. You should know what to wear as a tourist guide if you are trying to be as professional as you should be. Which of the following clothing is impropriate for you?

    A. Clothing with negative messages

    B. Tailored trousers or skirt for ladies

C. Smart sweaters

D. Jacket

5. Which of the following statement is incorrect?

A. It is far better to refer the tourist to a manager of the scenic area than to make up an answer or have a wide guess

B. Tourist guides shall not in any way compel or attempt to compel visitors to make purchases, or mislead or attempt to mislead them into doing so

C. Tourist guides shall not allow their service attitude to be affected nor shall they refuse to perform their duties because of visitors' unwillingness to purchase or the value of their purchases

D. Tourist guides can arrange self-pay activities for visitors without the approval by their travel agent

Group Discussion

Recently a mainland visitor was reportedly dissatisfied with the attitude of the tourist guide while shopping at a registered shop. He felt unwell later and was taken to Queen Elizabeth Hospital, where he was certified dead. Whether the tourist guide, the registered shop and the receiving agent concerned have violated any rules or pledges is now under thoroughly investigation. As the investigation is still ongoing, details of the case cannot be disclosed. If there is any suspected violation of rules or pledges, the case will be handled by the Compliance Committee or the Committee on Shopping-related Practices in accordance with established procedures.

(Source: http://www.tichk.org/public/website/en/news/2010_06_01/html.)

1. What measures should be taken to prevent this severe nature of the incident?

2. Please discuss the negative impacts of this incident to the image of Hong Kong tourism industry.

Guiding Exercise

As scheduled, you are taking a group of German tourists to visit the Shu Embroidery Handicrafts Factory. You are supposed to briefly introduce your visiting plan, and remind them what to do and what not to do when visiting, such as how long to stay, no smoking, etc.

Upon arriving, Miss Hu, an on-site guide shows the group around while making commentaries. You are supposed to do interpretation when tourists are purchasing. One of the tourists, Jason is interested in a jade bracelet rather than Shu Embroidery. He wants to buy the bracelet for his girl friend. As he has no experience of buying jade before, he will come to you and ask if the jade with the price of 2 000 Yuan is too expensive.

One hour later, when almost everyone has purchased what they like and you are supposed to go back to the hotel, the Green couples are absent. With the help of Miss Hu and tour leader, the couples are found, resulting complaints from the rest.

Translation Exercise

1. Please translate the following passage into Chinese.

Situated in eastern Asia, and on the western shore of the Pacific Ocean, the People's Republic of China covers a land area of 9.6 million square kilometers, with an inland and coastal water area of more than 4.7 million square kilometers and an eastern and southern continental coastline extending for about 18 000 kilometers. Its vast maritime territory is studded with 7 600 islands, of which Taiwan is the largest with an area of 35 798 square kilometers. China shares common borders with 14 countries and is adjacent to 8 nations on the ocean. There are 4 municipalities directly under central government administration, 23 provinces, 5 autonomous regions and 2 special administrative regions. The capital city is Beijing.

2. Please translate the following passage into English.

道教奉老子为教祖，把《道德经》作为主要经典，以"道"为最根本的信仰，一切教理教义都由此而衍化产生。道教认为"道"无所不包，无所不在，是一切的开始。与道并提的是"德"，所以道教规定信徒要"修道养德"，追求与道合一，与自然、社会和谐。因此，道和德就是道教的核心和基本的教义。

Case Study

游客一行10人在北京参加了众星旅游社组织的武夷山4日游。按照行程，6月5日下午为游客自由活动时间，但导游吴某将游客带到了一家珠宝店，这里的所有卖品都不给出成分和价签，一个"时来运转"吊坠的成交价竟达1 000元，而正规金店只卖500元。最可气的是因为10人总共只买了2 000元的商品，没有达到商店规定的最低消费金额，商店人员竟然不让游客出门。游客随即向吴某求助，但此时已经找不到吴某的踪迹。最后还是一个女团友又消费了1 000元商店人员才勉强放行。游客回到北京之后将旅行社及导游吴某投诉至当地旅游主管部门。

1. 在该案例中导游员及旅行社应该受到怎样的处罚？
2. 游客应该如何保护自己的合法权益不受侵害？

Further Reading

About the Guild

The Guild is the national professional association for Blue Badge Tourist Guides working throughout the British Isles. With around 700 full members and a network of regional and local associations with nearly 1 000 members holding group membership, the Guild represents around 1 700 guides. Its members offer guiding in 34 different languages. They are listed in the Guide Search facility.

Since its foundation in 1950, the Guild has been dedicated to raising and maintaining the highest professional standards of its membership. The Blue Badge is recognized internationally as the qualification of excellence in site and heritage interpretation, and in communication skills. It is awarded only by the following extensive training and vigorous examination.

The Guild is run by an Executive Council, elected by the membership, and salaried office staff, and provides support and advice to its members on both policy and all issues covering guide services, sites, coach operators and health & safety.

The members are kept up-to-date with Guide Post, a monthly newsletter packed with informative articles and updates on guiding-related issues; monthly diaries listing major events, opening times and admission prices; access to an extensive Continuing Professional Development programme.

Guild members are covered under public liability insurance, which provides annual cover up to £5million. A copy of the policy is kept at Guild House and the office staff can assist with any enquiries you have as to extent of cover, which includes cover whilst on tour anywhere in the world.

As a highly respected organization within the tourism industry the Guild is without political bias. It acts as a pressure group and consultative body on all matters concerning guiding. Members of the industry who become one of our preferred partners receive monthly information on events and openings, plus a variety of initiatives – for details phone our office on 020 7403 1115.

The Guild is a member of FEG, which acts to bring together and strengthen professional tourist guiding links and standards across Europe, and WFTGA, the international forum for tourist guides.

The Guild devotes major resources to guide training in its role as a training provider accredited by the Institute of Tourist Guiding. It is currently running two courses for Blue Badge Guides in London (78 trainees).

Due to its extensive experience of training, the Guild played a major role in the creation of the Institute of Tourist Guiding in 2002. The Institute is a government-recognized body responsible for setting standards within the tourist-guiding sector. It accredits training courses and sets examinations for entry into all levels of the profession and is also the registering authority for Blue Badge Tourist Guides in the United Kingdom (except Scotland). Guild members sit on the member-elected body of trustees.

(Source from: http://www.britainsbestguides.org/)

Chapter 8

Presentation Techniques

Learning Outcome

After reading this chapter, you will be able to:

- Understand how to project voice loudly and clearly
- Recognize different levels of diction
- Know how to use microphone correctly
- Be aware of the basic breathing techniques
- Realize the importance of eye contact and body language
- Understand how to present clear and accurate information and clearly give directions for visible objects by word and gesture
- Learn to use speech that is appropriate and in varied manner, pace, style and vocabulary
- Identify the required language skills for guiding tourists

Opening Case

The first ASEAN Tourist Guide Contest was held in Yogyakarta, Indonesia, 24~28 September 2011. The opening ceremony took place at the Sultan Palace in Yogyakarta and was attended by His Highness  Sri Paku Alam as the Vice Governor of Yogyakarta. Delegates were also taken to the UNESCO heritage sites Borobudur and Prambanan Temple.

The main objective for the contest is to share knowledge and guiding experiences among colleagues. The guiding curriculum was called ASEAN Common Competency Standard for Tourism Professionalism. Delegates were judged on aspects of guiding technique, performance, knowledge of destination, communication skills, English and information technology. Roger Rajah from Malaysia did an excellent job as chair of the jury. 18 delegates from Laos, Myanmar, Cambodia, Vietnam, Thailand, Malaysia, Singapore, Indonesia and Brunei Darussalam took part. The winner was Diana Chua from Singapore, runner-up was Anne Molly from Malaysia, and Uji Gaffar from Indonesia came third.

The Ministry for Culture and Tourism (sponsors of the event) and the ASEAN secretariat were impressed with this contest and will support the second SEATGA contest in Thailand 2013.

(Source: Guidelines Internetion@l, Issue No. Issue 17 February 2012.)

Chapter 8

1. What is the main objective for the contest?
2. Do you have any interest in taking part in the Contest? And why?

Introduction

In tour guiding, a presentation would be introducing the place or the country in terms of its importance and history, politics, culture and nature to the participants of the tour. This can be done as part of the motor coach ride or simply on-site. For an on-site tourist guide, the vocal delivery is even more important. Presentation in this aspect is also called a tour commentary, which is usually referred to as "guidespeak".

As long as the ability to give brief presentation is a learned skill, in this chapter, we will learn how to master this skill by discussing voice projection, diction and microphone use, eye contact and body language, personal appearance and behavior, style and vocabulary, and required language skills.

Presentation Techniques 153

8.1 Voice Projection, Diction, Microphone Use, Breathing Techniques

8.1.1 Voice Projection

Voice *projection* is the strength of speaking or singing whereby the voice is used loudly and clearly. It is a technique that can be employed to demand respect and attention. Whether you are an on-site tourist guide or speaking on a bus, effective voice projection is essential if you want people to hear you clearly and take you seriously as a speaking guide.

Strong voices are necessary for professional tourist guides who need to project their voices in various situations and *arenas*. It is important for tourist guides to be heard clearly and vividly, even without microphone. Effective voice projection depends on a combination of 3 key areas: breathing technique, *resonance* and *pitch*.

With practice and the right techniques, you can learn how to be more effective by improving your voice projection. There are plenty of exercises to develop all of these areas, but here are a few which, if practiced regularly, will really make a difference to the way your voice sounds and travels: you'll be heard at the back of a busy room without resorting to shouting. The following are some instructions for tourist guide to practice using voice correctly with a variety of pitch and tone:

- Practice relaxation exercises before speaking.
- Loosen up your tongue when you are going to be saying many tricky phrases.
- Practice altering the pitch of your voice.
- Breath technique is essential for proper voice projection.
- Ensure that you can be heard by the whole group;
- Be aware of your colleagues and the environment and **modulate** the volume accordingly when using the natural voice project your voice;
- Make use of natural features to project sound e.g. "walls";
- Find areas where there is protection from noise, where appropriate;
- Vary your pitch and tone for emphasis and to maintain interest;
- Avoid lowering the tone of your voice at the end of sentences;
- Use a lively tone.

Besides, there are some other Tips & Warnings when practicing projecting your voice:

- Keep vocal cords healthy by limiting alcohol consumption;
- Smoking will affect your voice, so it's definitely better not to smoke at all;
- Avoid tea, coffee and other drinks that contain **caffeine**;
- Don't drink cold water right before a performance;
- Avoid rooms with dry air before an acting job;
- Avoid overusing your voice;
- The more confident you are, the stronger your voice will be.

8.1.2 Diction

The Merriam-Webster dictionary defines "diction" as simply your choice of words especially with regard to correctness, clearness, or effectiveness. There is no single, correct diction in the English language; instead, you choose different words or phrases for different contexts:

- To a friend — "a screw-up";
- To a child —"a mistake";

- To the police —"an accident";
- To an employer — "an oversight".

All of these expressions mean the same thing, that is, they have the same **denotation** but you would not likely switch one for the other in any of these three situations: a police officer or employer would take "screw-up" as an insult, while your friends would take "oversight" as an **affectation**.

Diction will be effective only when the words you choose are appropriate for the audience and purpose, when they convey your message accurately and comfortably. The idea of comfort may seem out of place in connection with diction, but, in fact, words can sometimes cause the listener to feel uncomfortable (Martha Kolln, 1999).

Sometimes diction is described in terms of 4 levels of language: ①formal, as in serious **discourse**; ②informal, as in relaxed but polite conversation; ③*colloquial*, as in everyday usage; ④ **slang**, as in impolite and newly coined words (Jack Myers, Don Charles Wukasch, 2003).

Some people seem to think that when it comes to word choice, "bigger is always better". However, using a word just because it is big is a bad idea. You're better off using words for their exactness, appropriateness, and accuracy than for their size. The only time a bigger word is a better choice is when it is more accurate. In any case, the final decision to use this word over that should be based on the audience for whom you're speaking (Anthony C. Winkler, Jo Ray Metherell, 2012)

8.1.3 Microphone Use

A microphone is a tool to amplify your voice, not a substitute for good vocal expression. It won't make a boring voice interesting—just louder. So, learn the techniques of good microphone use.

Knowledge Links [8-1]

> 麦克风的头朝天，这样采集的音色会强调低音。如果声音比较尖的导游员可以平拿麦克风，这样麦克风采集的音色最为丰富，但在发/b/、/p/等爆破音时易引起"喷"话筒。在讲话时可以将麦克风朝右边或右上，这样采集的音色会强调高音，适宜于声音低沉或是高音很有特色的导游。持麦克风的距离会影响音量的变化，最好先讲几句客套话来试试音量，找到合适的距离。

When you use a microphone, you still have to use your full voice to engage your audience and establish your identity as a speaker. Under the pressure of presenting before an audience, a speaker can lose natural vocal expression. As you *rehearse*, experiment with volume, pitch, and rhythm to achieve *optimal* expression and emphasis. By varying your volume, pitch, and rhythm, you'll be able to convey meaning and emotion. Without variation, your voice will sound boring, *monotonous*, and *robotic*. Use vocal diversity to make sure your audience understands and feels the tone of your message.

The following are tips for using microphone correctly when coaching a tour:

- Check that the microphone is switched on and working;
- Adjust volume for clarity and *interference*;
- Adjust position of microphone for clarity, volume and interference;
- Check that everyone can hear;
- Ensure that you are not speaking too loudly for the microphone and adjust the position of the microphone according to feedback from the group;
- Keep the microphone with you while talking and gesturing and do not allow contact to be lost;
- Avoid walking up the coach with the microphone

8.1.4 Breathing Techniques

Breathing technique is essential for proper voice projection. Good voice projection requires efficient working of the lungs, *intercostal* muscles and *diaphragm*.

Place one hand on your belly and another hand on your back. Breathe in slowly, and feel the gap between your hands get wider as your belly moves outward. Take a few deep breaths in and out, and feel the hand on your belly moving out and in as you do so. Now place your hands, with fingertips touching, across your belly, just below the *ribcage*. Breathe in and feel your belly move out, then breathe out making a hard, quick "huh" sound — you should feel your belly contract as the sound comes out. Repeat several times.

Practice this *abdominal* breathing regularly so that it becomes normal and natural anywhere. Then try making different sounds. Hear how much stronger and clearer the voice is, and how much more it projects when you breathe abdominally.

8.2 Eye Contact and Body Language

8.2.1 Eye Contact

Eye contact is an important aspect of social interaction, and it is something that many shy and socially anxious people have difficulty with. Fortunately, most people can learn to overcome this fear and maintain better eye contact, a key aspect of effective communication with tourists.

Some simple tricks will help you maintain great eye contact during walking and on-site tours include:

- As you start to practice matching your tourist's eye contact, you'll start to develop a sense of how much eye contact feels "natural". When your tourist looks at you, look at them; When they look away, look away; Pause for a few seconds before matching your tourist's eye contact.
- Be aware of cultural differences. Some cultures consider making direct eye contact aggressive, rude, or a show of disrespect. Other cultures, and some religious groups, consider eye contact between men and women inappropriate and either as threatening. A good case in point is that "do not impose eye contact on Japanese visitors".
- Stand up and face the group while making the introduction and scan the group to ensure that you look at all the members of the group.
- Do not turn away while gesturing at objects, buildings or areas.
- Focus attention on the whole group, do not leave anyone out.
- Instead of thinking of the group as a whole, imagine that you are having individual conversations with one person in the group at a time.
- Choose a spot directly between or slightly above the listener's eyes. If this doesn't feel comfortable, try letting your eyes go slightly out of focus. This has the added benefit of softening and relaxing your gaze.

Knowledge Links [8-2]

> 导游口试采用室内模拟方式。模拟场景空间为两个：一为景区，一为旅途（旅游车内）。模拟形式：景点现场讲解，途中车内导游，游客提问回答。口试着重测试地陪服务最核心的导游讲解能力，细项涵盖语言表达（外语类增加个人展示和口译）、仪表礼仪、音质音量、语感语速、模拟途中讲解的

> 形式及内容、模拟景点讲解的形式及内容、知识问答等测试项目，全面检验应试人员的基本功和专业素质。外语口试增加个人展示（自我介绍或对导游工作的认识或感悟）和口译（汉语译外语、外语翻汉语，均用口语对话完成）题目2个，汉—外、外—汉各1个。

8.2.2 Body Language

The Oxford English Dictionary (revised 2005) defines 'body language' as the conscious and unconscious movements and postures by which attitudes and feelings are communicated.

Body language as a form of non-verbal communication is not just about how we hold and move our bodies. It potentially, although not always, encompasses:

- How we position our bodies;
- Our closeness to and the space between us and other people, and how this changes;
- Our facial expressions;
- Our eyes especially and how our eyes move and focus;
- How we touch ourselves and others;
- How our bodies connect with other non-bodily things, for instance, pens, cigarettes, *spectacles* and clothing;
- Our breathing, and other less noticeable physical effects, for example our heartbeat and perspiration;

This following is just a summary of the most interesting definitions of body language:

Active listening: listening very attentively, empathizing, and reflecting back understanding through body language and usually words too.

Alerting gestures: indicating need to speak, for example raising a hand, or taking a breath and lifting the shoulders.

Barrier: describing signals in which the hands or arms form a defense or *obstruction* between two people, such as folded arms.

Displacement: a stress signal typically prompted by suppression of natural reaction due to fear or other *inhibition*, for example biting fingernails, picking at finger(s) or thumb.

Eyebrow flash: quickly raising and lowering both eyebrows, typically in greetings, recognition, acknowledgment, or surprise. An eyebrow flash can therefore also be a signal of positive interest.

Eye shrug: upwards eyes roll signaling frustration.

Face frame: framing the face with the hands to hold or attract listeners' attention.

8.3 Style and Vocabulary

8.3.1 Present Clear and Accurate Information

- Do not read notes, although you may have them with you;
- Be careful not to assume knowledge to the visitor;
- Research information and be accurate about dates, place and facts;
- If telling a story or anecdote, say that it is a story or one version of a story;

- Make sure that your presentation is planned and logical and *chronological*, a story needs a beginning, a body and an end.

8.3.2 Clearly give directions for visible objects by word and/or gesture

- Do not talk about things once you have passed them if you miss something, so leave it out.
- In the coach, give clear indication of important sites just before reaching them and give clear directions when they are within sight.
- Avoid pointing out things that cannot be seen by the entire group.
- Use colors, signs, materials or larger objects to make things clear e.g. The building with the red roof; when on foot clearly point to the building, object or area that you want them to see.
- Use meaningful hand gestures.

8.3.3 Present Speech Appropriately

- Use speech that is appropriate and in a varied manner on pace, style and vocabulary.
- Use correct pronunciation.
- Use clear simple language; slow down from normal speech: the larger the group, the slower the speech; *articulate* clearly.
- Avoid or explain jargon or technical vocabulary.
- Make place names clear and if necessary spell them.
- Avoid over used phrases e.g. "over there, on the right, at 1 o'clock".
- Be enthusiastic and use your sense of humor.
- Avoid negative or suggestive language.

- Avoid making judgments or stating personal opinions on controversial subjects.

8.4 Required Language Skills

Although tourist guide does not have to be multi-lingual, in social and travel contexts, users at this level are beyond the stage of having any problems in dealing with many of the routine situations of everyday life, such as those which arise in shops, restaurants, banks and hotels.

Knowledge Links [8-3]

> 导游口试的一般流程：1.考生进入考场，交验准考证和身份证；2.考生自选旅游线路进行"途中模拟导游"；3.讲解完毕由评委模拟游客提问，不超过两个问题，考生回答；4.提问完毕，考生抽签。根据所抽题签限定的旅游片区，在规定片区范围内自选一个景点进行讲解；4.讲解完毕，评委模拟游客提问，不超过两个问题，考生回答；5.提问回答完毕，考试结束，考生退出考场。

Range: has a good command of a broad range of language allowing him/her to express him/herself clearly in an appropriate style on a wide range of general, academic, professional or leisure topics without having to restrict what he/she wants to say.

Accuracy: consistently maintains a high degree of grammatical accuracy;

errors are rare and generally corrected when they do occur.

Fluency: express him/herself fluently and ***spontaneously***, almost effortlessly. Only a conceptually difficult subject can hinder a natural, smooth flow of language.

Interaction: select a suitable phrase from a readily available range of discourse functions to preface his/her remarks in order to get or keep the floor and to relate his/her own contributions skillfully to those of other speakers.

Coherence: produce clear, smoothly flowing, well-structured speech, showing controlled use of organizational patterns, connectors and cohesive devices.

Summary

Summary

A presentation enables tourist guide to show himself as a leader and the one responsible for the group. In this chapter, we have discussed how to grasp presentation as a learned skill.

It begins with the instructions and tips/warnings for voice projection. After clarifying what diction is, it goes to teach how to use microphone correctly and abdominal breathing technique essential for proper voice projection. Then, it moves to deal with tricks of eye contact and to introduce some most frequently used body languages as a form of non-verbal communication. After that, personal appearance and behavior have been addressed. The last two parts talk about style and vocabulary, as well as required language skills to guide tourists.

Key Words and Phrases

Projection /prəˈdʒekʃ(ə)n/ *noun*: the act or process of causing a picture, movie, etc., to appear on a surface.

Arena /əˈriːnə/ *noun*: a building for sports and other forms of entertainment that has a large central area surrounded by seats.

Resonance /ˈrezənəns/ *noun*: a sound or vibration produced in one object that is caused by the sound or vibration produced in another.

Pitch /ˈpitʃ/ *noun*: the highness or lowness of a sound.

Modulate /ˈmɒdjʊleit/ *verb*: to change the sound of (your voice) by making it quieter, higher, lower, etc..

Caffeine /kæˈfiːn, ˈkæˌfiːn/ *noun*: a substance that is found especially in coffee and tea and that makes you feel more awake.

Denotation /ˌdiːnəʊˈteɪʃ(ə)n/ *noun*: the meaning of a word or phrase.

Affectation /ˌæfekˈteɪʃ(ə)n/ *noun*: an unnatural form of behavior that is meant to impress others.

Discourse /ˈdɪskɔːs, -ˈkɔːrs/ *noun*: the use of words to exchange thoughts and ideas.

Colloquial /kəˈləʊkwɪəl/ *adjective*: used when people are speaking in an informal way.

Slang /ˈslæŋ/ *noun*: words that are not considered part of the standard vocabulary of a language and that are used very informally in speech especially by a particular group of people.

Rehearse /rɪˈhɜːs/ *verb*: to prepare for a public performance of a play, a piece of music, etc., by practicing the performance.

Optimal /ˈɒptɪm(ə)l/ *adjective*: best or most effective.

Monotonous /məˈnɒt(ə)nəs/ *adjective*: used to describe something that is boring because it is always the same.

Robotic /rəʊˈbɒtɪk/ *adjective*: someone who is robotic acts like a robot by making stiff movements, not showing any human feelings etc..

Interference /ˌɪntəˈfɪər(ə)ns/ *noun*: additional signals that weaken or block the main signal in a radio or television broadcast.

Intercostal /ˌɪntəˈkɒst(ə)l/ *adjective*: between the ribs (=bones around the chest).

Diaphragm /ˈdaɪəˌfræm/ *noun*: a large flat muscle that separates the lungs from the stomach area and that is used in breathing.

Ribcage /rɪbkeɪdʒ/ *noun*: the curved wall of ribs that surrounds and protects the chest.

Abdomen /ˈæbdəmən/ *noun*: the part of the body below the chest that contains the stomach and other organs.

Spectacle /'spektəkl/ *noun*: an unusual or unexpected event or situation which attracts attention, interest or disapproval.

Empathizie /'empəˌθaiz/ *verb*: to have the same feelings as another person; to feel empathy for someone — often + with.

Obstruction /əb'strʌkʃ(ə)n/ *noun*: something that blocks something else and makes it difficult for things to move through.

Inhibition /ˌin(h)i'biʃ(ə)n/ *noun*: a nervous feeling that prevents you from expressing your thoughts, emotions, or desires.

Chronological /ˌkrɒ:nə'lɒ:dʒɪk(ə)l/ *adjective*: arranged in the order that things happened or came to be.

Articulate /ˌkrɒ:nə'lɒ:dʒɪk(ə)l/ *adjective*: able to express ideas clearly and effectively in speech or writing.

Spontaneous /ɑ'tikjʊlət/ *adjective*: done or said in a natural and often sudden way and without a lot of thought or planning.

Review Questions

1. Discuss how to project voice loudly and clearly.
2. Discuss how to use microphone correctly.
3. Practice abdominal breathing techniques.
4. Practice eye contact and body language.
5. Retell how to dress and behave appropriately for the occasion.
6. Practice the skill of presenting clear and accurate information and clearly giving directions for visible objects by word and or gesture.
7. Discuss the required language skills for guiding tourists.

Choice Questions

Choose the best answer to the questions below. You need to correctly answer 3 of the 5 questions to pass.

1. Which of the following statement is incorrect for using microphone?

A. Check that the microphone is switched on and working

B. Adjust position of microphone for clarity, volume and interference

C. Keep the microphone with you while talking and gesturing and do not allow contact to be lost

D. Speak as loudly as you can to make everyone hear

2. Which of the following should be avoided as a professional tourist guide when showing directions?

A. Use meaningful hand gestures

B. Point out things that cannot be seen by all the group

C. Give clear directions when they are within sight

D. Use colors, signs, materials or larger objects to make things clear

3. Some cultures consider making direct eye contact aggressive, rude, or a show of disrespect. A good case in point is:

A. Impose eye contact on Germany visitors

B. Impose eye contact on British visitors

C. Impose eye contact on American visitors

D. Impose eye contact on Japanese visitors

4. How to define "accuracy"?

A. Produce clear, smoothly flowing, well-structured speech, showing controlled use of organizational patterns, connectors and cohesive devices

B. Express him/herself fluently and spontaneously, almost effortlessly. Only a conceptually difficult subject can hinder a natural, smooth flow of language

C. Consistently maintains a high degree of grammatical accuracy; errors are rare and generally corrected when they do occur

D. Select a suitable phrase from a readily available range of discourse functions to preface his/her remarks in order to get or keep the floor and to relate his/her own contributions skillfully to those of other speakers

5. Diction will be effective only when the words you choose are appropriate for the audience and purpose, when they convey your message accurately and comfortably.

A. True

B. False

Group Discussion

The China National Tourism Administration announced on its official website that the Regulation on Tourist Complaints Handling had been put in force from July 1, 2010.

According to the document, the statute of limitation for tourist complaints will be extended to 90 days, 30 days longer than the trial Interim Regulations on Tourist Complaints. On receiving complaints from tourists, the related tourism quality supervision departments should handle these within five working days, while respondents should make a written reply in ten days after receiving notices. The complaints handling body should issue a "tourist complaint mediation letter" if the complainant and respondent have reached a mediated agreement in 60 days; if not, complainants could apply for arbitration or file a lawsuit.

The document also has provisions about the use of a travel agency quality bond in case tourists are stranded. If there is loss of tourists' prepaid expense or if tourists are stranded due to a travel agency's behavior, the agency should pay the costs of transport, accommodation or a return trip in a timely manner.

If tourists can not reach a mediated settlement with an agency, the complaint handling body can make the decision to transfer the agency's quality bond to compensate the tourists, or it can make a suggestion to the tourism administrative department on the transfer of the quality bond.

(Source: http://english.cri.cn/6566/2010/05/26/902s572260.htm.)

1. Discuss the benefits that the Regulation on Tourist Complaints Handling brings to tourists.

2. If you were a manager of a local travel agent, what would you like to say about the regulation?

Guiding Exercise

You are travelling with a group of tourists from America to visit Wuhou Temple in Chengdu. As a local tourist guide, you are supposed to provide a commentary. The following is just an example of what you are going to say when you arrive at the site. Please use the presentation techniques we have discussed in this chapter to make an interesting and memorable commentary.

Good morning/afternoon, Ladies and Gentlemen,

Now we are here at the front gate of the Wuhou temple.

The temple is located at the south urban area of Chengdu. It is a famous historical site dedicated to the memorial of both Liu Bei (161—223), Emperor of the Shu in the Three Kingdoms Period (220—280), and Zhuge Liang (181—234), Prime Minister of the Shu.

If you have read the popular classical Chinese novel The Romance of the Three Kingdoms, which has been translated into many languages including English, you will definitely be very familiar with the history of the Three Kingdoms Period.

After the Eastern Han Dynasty collapsed in the early 3rd century, the period of Three Kingdoms period arose. At that time, China was divided into three kingdoms, i.e. the Kingdom of Wei, Shu (also known as Shuhan), and Wu. They competed to reunify the country, leaving behind tales of heroism and remains, among which many are located in Sichuan.

Sitting on the central axis, the whole complex faces south direction with the First Gate, the Second gate, the Hall of Liu Bei, the Corridor, and the Hall of Zhuge Liang.

You may notice that a board hung above the First Gate reads "Han Zhao Lie Temple", implying that such a temple was set up in honor of Liu Bei, for Zhao Lie was the title given to Liu Bei after his death. In spite of this, the temple is commonly known as Wuhou Memorial Temple or Temple of Marquis Wu as Zhuge Liang was conferred on the title of "Zhong Wu Xiang Hou" or Marquis Wu after his death.

As a matter of fact, the Temple of Marquis Wu was first built by Li Xiong of the Western Jin Dynasty (265—316), 400 years after Zhuge Liang's death. It was not until the 14th century that the two were combined together into one. The buildings we have seen today were rebuilt in the Qing Dynasty in the 17th century. This Temple is the only historical temple in China that was built for both the king and his officer.

All right, let us get into the next hall. That is all, Thank you!

Translation Exercise

1. Please translate the following passage into Chinese.

The Ding Kiln started producing ceramics in the Tang Dynasty (618—907) and thrived during the Song (960—1279) and the Jurchen Jinn(1115—1234) dynasties. It phased out in the late Yuan Dynasty (1271—1368). The Ding kiln was celebrated for its white-glazed ceramic ware which is designed in decent shapes, coated with pure white and lustrous glaze, and primarily decorated with carved, incised, molded, or gold-tracery floral designs. Besides their large volume consumed by the multitudes, the Ding ware had been the major ceramic supplier for the imperial family and governments from late Tang Dynasty to the Jurchen Jinn Dynasty.

2. Please translate the following passage into English.

佛教是我国现有五大宗教中历史比较悠久、影响较大的一个宗教。在我国有2 000余年的历史。佛教虽然来自印度，但其成熟和发展是在中国完成的，它既吸收了中国传统文化，又丰富了中国传统文化。当代的中国佛教是传统的中国佛教的继承和延续，并随着社会历史、政治经济、科学文化、思想观念、生活方式的发展变化而发展变化。

Case Study

导游小李笨拙地拿起话筒，侧身靠着车门站定了。他打开话筒刚要开口说话，车顶上的扩音器发出不堪卒闻的刺耳的尖啸，以致游客们全都惊叫着用手捂住耳朵。小李不知道是怎么回事，一时手足无措，只好赶紧将话筒关上。他再次打开话筒，尖啸声再次像防空警报似的响起来。小李怯生生地问司机："陈师傅，这话筒是怎么回事呀？"司机扭头用海南式的普通话训斥道："把话筒拿好啰，别对着扩音器嘛。"

小李把话筒朝自己放平了一些，刺耳的尖啸果然就消失了。司机又用海南方言嘟哝了一句什么，许平生听不懂，但他猜得出，司机是在骂他这个导游笨，连话筒都不会拿。小李羞愧得满面通红。但此时此刻他没有时间难过，他在心里对自己说："比起韩信当年受人胯下之辱，司机的责骂算不了什么。我现在要为车上全体游客致欢迎辞，绝不能让旅游车上一开始就陷入冷场的尴尬境地。"他振作精神，鼓起勇气，声音洪亮地开始了他的首次导游讲解。

（资料来源：http://blog.sina.com.cn/s/blog_492a42ef010008i8.html.）

1. 指出小李在使用车载话筒中的不当之处。
2. 导游员应该如何正确使用车载话筒？

Further Reading

A Concise History of China (1)

Endowed with terra firma, China is reputed as one of the single oldest uninterrupted civilization in the world. A significant aspect of China is its long cultural and history. The Chinese have shared a common culture longer than any other group on Earth. The Chinese writing system dates back almost 4 000 years. The imperial dynastic system of government, which has continued for centuries, was established as early as 221 BC. Although certain dynasties were overturned, the dynastic system survived. Even when China was ruled at times by minority invaders, such as the Mongols during the Yuan Dynasty, from AD 1279 to 1368, the Manchus during the Qing Dynasty, from AD 1644 to 1911, the invaders were largely absorbed into the culture they governed.

It was in 1911 that the dynastic system was overturned, and a weak republican form of government existed until 1949. After the founding of the People's Republic of China in the year of 1949, the culture and power of China become much stronger, and China's role in the world economic and political affairs grew increasingly more important.

Chinese Stone Age Archaeological evidence suggests that China is one of the cradles of the human race. The first primitive man so far known to have existed in China is Yuanmou man, who lived about 1.7 million years ago. The famous Peking man lived approximately 400 000~500 000 years ago. The first people lived in caves, made fires, used stone and bone tools, and wore fur and leather clothes. They were hunters and gatherers. The gradual formation of matriarchal commune took place approximately 40 000 or 50 000 years ago, and the patriarchal commune appeared more than 5 000 ago.

As in Egypt and West Asia, the first place where Chinese people began farming was in a river valley, along the Yellow River in northern China.

Once the Chinese began farming, they also began to live in villages. With rough tools they build small houses with reed roofs and made pottery. Two kinds of Chinese pottery from this time are very well known: red clay pots with swirling black designs from north-west China, and smooth black pots from north-east China.

According to traditional ideas, the first dynasty that appeared in Chinese history was the Xia, which ruled for more than 400 years. It is generally thought that the Xia lasted from 21 century BC to 16 century BC. However, we still lack some evidence to prove its existence. Archaeologists are trying hard to find out the truth about the Xia.

The first dynasty that can be traced from archaeological discoveries and from records was the Shang, having begun some 3 600 years ago. According to legends, the Shang Dynasty traced its origin to an ancient tribe on the lower reaches of Huanghe (the Yellow River).

Around 16 century BC, the Shang Dynasty had united a big part of China under one king. The king had his capital in Anyang, in northern China. China had entered the stage of slave society. Under such a condition, people had already begun to divide up into the rich and the poor.

People also used jade (a green stone) for jewelry and decoration. At that time, the Chinese learned how to make bronze out of tin and copper, so we call this the Bronze Age. About the same time, based on pictures that stand for ideas or sounds, they developed writing system. We know of this writing from oracle bones, which are bones with writing carved into them. They were used to tell fortunes. People also used bones and tortoise shells to keep records. The Shang Dynasty lasted for about 700 years. But finally they were conquered by the Zhou.

The Zhou conquered the Shang Dynasty at about 1100 BC. The Zhou kings called themselves "sons of heaven," and their success in overcoming the Shang was seen as the "mandate of the heaven". The long period of the Zhou Dynasty is divided into 2 sub periods: Western and Eastern Zhou, named for the locations of the capitals.

In 771 BC, China was invaded by skillful fighters from the northwest. The Zhou emperors retreated and moved from the older one at Haojing to the new capital at Luoyang further east. So this period is called the Eastern Zhou, lasting from 770 to 221BC.

The first 300 years of the Eastern Zhou period is called the Spring and Autumn period. Iron began to be used for tools in China at this time. But iron also made good weapons, and the 200 or so small states fought with each other all the time.

The period from 481 to 221 BC is called the Warring States period. By 256 BC, the Zhou emperors lost power, and the only rulers in China were the kings of the only 7 great states left. These kings fought among themselves until the king of Qin, the most powerful one, succeeded in making himself emperor and established the Qin Dynasty.

The Qin Dynasty is the one that gave its name to China. The first Qin emperor, in 221 BC, was Qinshihuang. To show that he was the emperor, and more important than the other kings, he built grand palaces and had very elaborate court ceremonies in his capital city of Xianyang. And, to show that the whole China belonged to just one empire now, Qin made everyone use the same letters to write and use the same measurements.

Qin also got together a huge army to keep its former rivals from revolting against him. In addition, when he didn't need it for smashing revolts, he kept the army busy defending the empire and making it more and more powerful. Soon China covered a vast area, from Mongolia in the north to Vietnam in the south. His most dangerous enemy were hunter races living in Mongolia and Siberia, who invaded the inner land of China. For defending themselves, former kingdoms had constructed walls along their northern borders. But Qin ordered his army to join up all these walls to make the Great Wall of China. The Great Wall Stretched 1 500 miles long (2 400 kilometers), and it still is spectacular!

Qinshihuang was buried in a huge tomb, with thousands of life-size clay soldiers to accompany him to the next world (the English name is the Terracotta Warriors or Statues). His successor was, unfortunately, a cruel yet cowardly young man, totally unable to rule his empire. Months after his succession, rebellions spread across the whole of China. Within just four years, Qin's well-known invincible army was defended. Its capital, Xianyang, was burned to the ground. Then, two rebel leaders, Xiang Yu and Liu Bang, fought over who would be the next emperor.

Gaozu (Liu Bang) established the Han Dynasty in 202 BC and didn't really change that much of the system that Qin had set up. But Gaozu didn't kill or exile the scholars anymore. Instead, smart educated men were called to work for him, to be his governors or judges. This earlier part of the Han Dynasty is called the Western Han, because the capital was in Western China, at Chang'an. In 141 BC, Wudi, the Martial Emperor, succeeded the throne. During his reign, military campaigns against the Huns or the Xiong-Nu were successfully carried out; the first university in China was set up in 124 BC. Students were taught Confucian philosophy and the official state philosophy there.

In 9 AD, a man named Wang Mang, who was a nephew of then Han empress, usurped the throne and called his new dynasty the Xin Dynasty. Wang Mang took over power by promising to transport much power and land from the rich to the poor. But this turned out to be a mountainous lie. In 17 AD, the Red Eyebrows in East China began to launch their major attack on Wang Mang. Defeated by the poor, Wang Mang lost his life in 23 AD. 2 years later, a Han

Dynasty emperor took control of China again. His name was Liu Xiu (entitled as Guangwudi after his death). The Easter Han Dynasty moved its capital eastward to Luoyang since Chang'an had been devastated by war. In 73 AD, a great general, Ban Chao, went with an army of 70 000 men all the way across Asia to explore. He spent 28 years on his journey! After he got back, he was so knowledgeable that he was even able to tell the emperor certain details about the Roman Empire. The Han people, the major ethnic group in China, were formed in the Qin and Han periods through the fusion of related tribes and ethnic groups. The name of the Han people is that of a great dynasty. In the last years of the Han Dynasty, the emperors were not so powerful, causing many fights for power among different parts of government and between the government and the poor in the countryside. In 184 AD and 190 AD the poor people rebelled too. The leaders of these rebellions ended up killing more than 2 000 of the bodyguards and destroying the capital city.

By 207 AD, General Cao Cao managed to get control of northern China for himself. After he died in 220 AD, his son decided to remove the last Han emperor, and rule on his own in northern China. Other generals, like him, took over other parts of China, so China was divided into 3 kingdoms, called Wei, Shu Han, and Wu.

Chapter 9

Communication Techniques

Learning Outcome

After reading this chapter, you will be able to:
- Understand the importance of interpersonal skills
- Have a positive attitude to stress
- Learn the basic techniques of relieving work stress
- Be aware of the value of time management
- Know how to manage your time

Opening Case

A man in his 70s from Anhui province, surnamed Yao, wrote to Hainan province governor Jiang Dingzhi, complaining about being insulted by his tourist guide on Hainan island for refusing to pay the extra cost to visit the scenic spots he was scheduled to. Later, the tourist guide "dumped" Yao to fend for himself in an unknown place.

To gain greater competitive edge and attract more tourists, many travel agencies have advertised economy package tours at lower-than-normal prices, making it barely profitable for agencies and tourist guides both. Therefore, their main means of making money is forcing tourists to visit self-funded scenic spots and shops. Many tourist guides are not even paid by their employer agencies and have to rely on commissions from scenic spots and shops where they cajole or coerce tourists to go.

For example, the money Yao paid to the travel agency in Anhui hardly covered his tickets to and from Hainan. That means, the Anhui agency "sold" the tourists to the Hainan agency, so the latter forced tourists like Yao to pay an extra 600 to 900 Yuan.

Such tours leave a sour taste in the mouth for a long time. Many tourists who choose package tours find their trips rather tiring, troublesome and less satisfying than they had expected. Everything seems to go wrong. They can only spend one hour or even less at one scenic spot, merely enough to take a brief look at the scenery, click some photographs and then board the bus heading for the next site. The process is repeated day in and day out across the country.

(Source: http://www.chinadaily.com.cn/opinion/2012-07/28/content_15625580.htm.)

1. Describe any ill-treated cases by tour operators or tourist guide that you know or have experienced.

2. Why many travel agencies have advertised economy package tours at lower-than-normal prices?

Introduction

The purpose of this chapter is to discuss 3 fundamental techniques that make a professional tourist guide. We will begin with interpersonal skills first, followed by stress management and time management.

9.1 Interpersonal Skills

The *interpersonal* skills are used by a person to properly interact with others. Being a part of various key guiding skills, the term generally refers to a tourist guide's ability to get along with tourists and others while getting the job done. Interpersonal skills include the habits, attitudes, manners, appearance, and behaviors tourist guide uses around other people, which affect how they get along with other people.

Tourist guides with interpersonal skills connect with other people *effortlessly*, they seem to know the right things to say and they make communication in general an easy process. Interpersonal skills are an asset in the workplace, and they're important for *maintaining* friendships.

The development of interpersonal skills begins early in life and is influenced by family, friends, and our observations of the world. Television and movies also influence this area, but most of these characteristics are passed by our parents or guardians. Some aspects of interpersonal skills are even inherited. Appearance and some personality traits are largely influenced by genes.

For those who want to improve their interpersonal skills, it is suggested to be aware of what they are like from the perspective of other people who interact with them. Habits they are unaware of, actions they think go unnoticed, and other things about them that might affect other people are impossible for them to change if they are not aware of them.

People who lack interpersonal skills can learn how to develop them. Interpersonal skills may include but are not limited to:

- Effective communication;
- Cooperation;
- Giving and receiving feedback, and feed-forward;
- Acceptance of diversity;
- Supporting and encouraging others;
- **_Inclusiveness;_**
- Problem solving;
- Negotiation;
- Conflict resolution.

Effectively demonstrate interpersonal skills means that the tourist guide will use their interpersonal skills in a *perceptive* manner. It is expected that the selected interpersonal skills will be used by the tourist guide. The impact on others may include but is not limited to:

- Improved group or team performance;
- More *cohesiveness*;
- Shared understanding of what the goal is and the plan to reach it;
- Improved success;
- Increased enjoyment or satisfaction;
- Better communication;
- Quality of teamwork;
- More encouragement and support amongst group or team members.

Training people to develop interpersonal skills is often just a case of reinforcing what they already know.

- Encourage positive body language. Positive body language starts with a smile and direct eye contact.
- Teach active listening. Teach people to restate in their own words what another person has said. This not only signals the speaker that he is being listened to, but it shows the speaker that the listener is genuinely trying to understand what he is saying.

Communication Techniques 181

- Encourage people to communicate clearly, and choose their words carefully so that the meaning is understood. For example, discuss the difference between "we will need to have an early start tomorrow morning" and "we will need to have an early start at 7:30 AM, tomorrow Morning". Although both statements have a similar meaning, the latter clearly indicates the exact time.
- Teach people to always ask questions. Asking questions is essential because communication isn't always perfect or infallible. Tell people that it's always okay to ask a follow-up question to clarify or check your understanding.
- Remind people to treat others like human beings. In the workplace, it's okay to congratulate people on an aspect of their personal lives or express concern within reason. It shows you're taking an interest in their lives. Keep up to date with the events of people's lives, and congratulate them on milestones like *anniversaries*, or show concern if someone is going through a difficult time.
- Promote the expression of appreciation and positivity. Teach people to find one positive and unique thing about everyone they work with and to tell each person. Remind people to always say "thanks" for jobs well done or solid efforts.

9.2 Stress Management

The truth is that you will be under great pressure since you will need to take lots of responsibilities and duties, and you will be probably exposed to varied degrees of risks on your journey, such as traffic accident, landslide, flooding, earthquake or disease, just name a few. At the same time, tourists rely on you, because you might be the only friend that they know on a strange land. Generally speaking, you should know where those stressors are from and learn how to *tackle* them in some positive ways.

Knowledge Links [9-1]

> 　　导游是个极具潜力的职业，是国家的形象大使，是人类文明的传播者。然而导游生存面临各种压力。导游不仅要接受旅行社近乎苛刻的利益约束，还需要承受游客的挑剔、指责，甚至引起投诉。另一方面，要求导游员提供周到、耐心、完美的服务。而社会对导游员的评价有失公正，也缺乏一种制度保障导游员起码的社会地位。一个导游员从年轻到老，没有固定工资，没有起码的生活保障。建立一个合理的制度体系，给导游员起码的生活保障和待遇，使导游员安心于本职工作，明确努力的空间和方向，从而使他们产生一种职业责任感和职业归属感，愉快生活，开心工作。
>
> （资料来源：常永翔.导游生存压力与导游管理制度改革研究[J]. 中国校外教育. 2009（9）.）

9.2.1 Types of Stressors

Stress is the body's physical response to a perceived threat. In other words, stress is a response to danger.

Situations that are considered ***stress provoking*** are known as stressors. Stress is not always a bad thing. Stress is simply the body's response to changes that create taxing demands. Many professionals suggest that there is a difference between what we perceive as positive stress, and distress, which refers to negative stress. In daily life, we often use the term "stress" to describe negative situations. This leads many people to believe that all stress is bad for you, which is not true.

Positive stress has the following characteristics:
- Motivates, focuses energy;
- Is short-term;
- Is perceived as within our coping abilities;
- Feels exciting;
- Improves performance.

In contrast, negative stress has the following characteristics:
- Causes anxiety or concern;
- Can be short or long-term;
- Is perceived as outside of our coping abilities;
- Feels unpleasant;
- Hampers performance;
- Can lead to mental and physical problems.

9.2.2 Sources of Stress

We can experience stress from 4 basic sources:

The Environment —the environment can bombard you with intense and competing demands to adjust. Examples of environmental stressors include weather, noise, crowding, pollution, traffic, unsafe and substandard housing, and crime.

Social Stressors — we can experience multiple stressors arising from the demands of the different social roles we occupy, such as parent, spouse, caregiver, and employee. Some examples of social stressors include deadlines, financial problems, job interviews, presentations, disagreements, demands for your time and attention, loss of a loved one, divorce, and co-parenting.

Physiological — situations and circumstances affecting our body can be experienced as physiological stressors. Examples of physiological stressors include rapid growth of *adolescence*, *menopause*, illness, aging, giving birth, accidents, lack of exercise, poor nutrition, and sleep disturbances.

Thoughts — your brain interprets and perceives situations as stressful, difficult, painful, or pleasant. Some situations in life are stress provoking, but it is our thoughts that determine whether they are a problem for us.

9.2.3 Stress Relieving Techniques

By understanding ourselves and our reaction to stress-provoking situations, we can learn to handle stress more effectively. In the most accurate meaning, stress management is not about learning how to avoid or escape the pressures and turbulence of modern living; it is about learning to appreciate how the body reacts to these pressures, and about learning how to develop skills which enhance the body's adjustment. To learn stress management is to learn about the mind-body connection and to the degree to which we can control our health in a positive sense.

Mindfulness — mindfulness is the quality of being fully engaged in the present moment, without over-thinking or analyzing the experience.

Thought Stopping Techniques — thought stopping involves concentrating on the unwanted thoughts and, after a short time, suddenly stopping and emptying the mind. The command "Stop" or a loud noise is generally used to interrupt the unpleasant thoughts.

Physical Techniques — some of the physical stress-busters are explained below: stretching exercise, breathing stretching exercise, *meditation*, visual imagery, diet, rest, laughter.

Behavioral Techniques — behavioral techniques include time management, positive thinking, reframing, ventilation and problem-solving.

Diversion Techniques — Diversion activities include such activities as engaging in a hobby, taking a nap, watching T.V., listening to music, and going out to a movie, etc.

Workplace Techniques — stress-busters specific to workplace include getting organized, delegating, being assertive and balancing work and personal time.

9.3 Time Management

Time management refers to the development of processes and tools that increase efficiency and productivity. In business, time management has morphed into everything from methodologies such as enterprise resource planning through consultant services such as professional organizers.

Time management strategies seek to make effective use of the time that you do have. To be effective you must modify the demands on your time. The approach to effective time management can be divided into 2 stages: identify values and set goals; develop mechanisms of effective time management.

One way to remember these 2 stages is: first, do the right things; then, do those things rightly. This approach highlights the fact that being efficient with your time is not necessarily a great time management strategy. If you are efficient with your time you may find that you have more time to do more things. However, if you haven't identified your values, you will just keep piling more and more things onto an already busy schedule without asking yourself if doing these things is the way you want to spend your time.

9.3.1 Identify Values and Set Goals

A value is something that is important to you. It is something that has worth and gives your life meaning. Values include such things as health, good friendships, career, travel, and being good to the environment. Too often, people spend time doing things that aren't important, which takes time away from meaningful activities. *Prioritizing* your activities based on your values increases your sense of purpose and contributes to better mental and physical health — and it can help reduce stress.

You may already be able to articulate your values. If you are not sure what they are, take some time to discover them. There are several tools that can help you with this process. One simple way is to review a list of values and to rank them.

Once you clear about your values, look at where you spend your time and identify if you are spending time doing things that you value. Work towards reducing — or even removing — the things you do that are not consistent with your values and replace them with meaningful, rewarding and satisfying activities. An additional benefit of clarifying your values is that if you are asked to do something (or feel that you "should" do something) that is not in line with your values, you can confidently decide to not spend your time there.

9.3.2 Develop Mechanisms of Effective Time Management

Once you are doing the things that are consistent with your values, you can examine how you are doing them and, if necessary, modify your approach so that you are more efficient with your time. The *mechanisms* are also useful when doing things that you are *obliged* to do such as work tasks. Some ways to make the most effective use of your time include:

- Be realistic — how much time will an activity take? Too often, people underestimate how much time an activity will take. To ensure that you have enough time. Add extra time to what you think something will take. For example, if you think it will take you 30 minutes to get to the airport, plan your time so that you have 50 minutes to get there.

- Plan out daily activities — the most popular way to plan out activities is to use an agenda. In order to be effective, you need to actually stick to the plan. Be sure to incorporate flexibility. For example, leave time between appointments in case one goes longer than expected. Also, build efficiency into your plan. For example, if you have 4 errands to run in 4 different places, do them in an order that minimizes the travel distance between each.

- Use a "to do" list — a "to do" list gives you a quick glance at what needs to be done. Prioritize each item on your list and work to get the most pressing items completed first. You can find templates for "to do" lists on the Internet. Type in "to do list template" in Google and choose among the many options. Look for a "to do" list with a column for "priority".

- Delegate — you don't need to do everything yourself. If possible, delegate tasks to others. Be sure to delegate appropriately, which means to the person who should be doing it is willing to as well as able to do it well.

- Take advantage of "wasted" time — an example of using wasted time is to catch up on reading while waiting at the doctor's office or while riding the bus or the metro.

- Manage interruptions — most people work best when they focus on one task at a time. Interruptions can break ***momentum***. Some ways to manage interruptions are reading your e-mail only a few times a day, closing your office or room door when you are working, and not answering the phone when you are working.

- Build organization skills — if you are well organized you can save a lot of time. Some examples include creating an efficient system for filing and retrieving paper and digital documents, as well as laying out your clothes-or making your lunch-the night before to save you time in the morning.

Summary

Summary

This chapter discusses 3 fundamental skills that make a professional tourist guide, namely interpersonal skills, stress management, and time management.

Interpersonal skill mainly involves cooperation, problem solving, negotiation and conflict resolution. It is interest to learn how tourist guide would effectively demonstrate interpersonal skills in a perceptive manner.

Tourist guides are facing various degrees of stress. It will be of great help if guides understand the source of stress, and more importantly, to learn how to relieve stress.

Lastly, it talks about the value of time management as well as some tips for better managing your busy working schedule.

Key Words and Phrases

Effortlessly /ˈefətlisli/ *adverb*: showing or needing little or no effort when doing sth.

Maintain /meinˈtein/ *verb*: to cause (something) to exist or continue without changing.

Inclusiveness /inˈkluːsivnis/ *noun*: the state of covering or including everything.

Perceptive /pəˈseptiv/ *adjective*: having or showing an ability to understand or notice something easily or quickly.

Cohesiveness /kəʊˈhiːsivnis/ *noun*: the state of closely united.

Anniversary /ˌæniˈvəsəri/ *noun*: a date that is remembered or celebrated because a special or notable event occurred on that date in a previous year.

Tackle /ˈtækəl/ *verb*: to deal with (something difficult).

Stress Provoking /ˈstres prəˈvəʊkɪŋ/ *adjective*: phrase: causing people to feel the stress.

Adolescence /ˌædəˈlesn̩s/ *noun*: the period of life when a child develops into an adult.

Menopause /ˈmenəpɔːz/ *noun*: the time when a woman stops menstruating.

Reframe /riˈfreim/ *verb*: to put (something) inside an open structure that holds it.

Ventilation /ˌventəˈleɪʃ(ə)n/ *noun*: open discussion or dispute over sth.

Assertive /əˈsətiv/ *adjective*: confident in behavior or style.

Prioritize /praɪˈɒrəˌtaiz/ *verb*: to organize (things) so that the most important thing is done or dealt with first.

Mechanism /ˈmek(ə)ˌnɪz(ə)m/ *noun*: a process or system that is used to produce a particular result.

Oblige /əˈblaɪdʒ/ *verb*: to force or require (someone or something) to do something because of a law or rule or because it is necessary.

Momentum /məˈmentəm/ *noun*: the strength or force that allows something to continue or to grow stronger or faster as time passes.

Review Questions

1. How to develop interpersonal skills?
2. What are the positive aspects of stress?
3. How to handle working stress?
4. How to manage your busy working schedule?

Choice Questions

Choose the best answer to the questions below. You need to correctly answer 3 of the 5 questions to pass.

Communication Techniques 191

1. Which of the following statement is not considered to be an effective interpersonal skill?

   A. Always say "thanks" for jobs well-done or solid efforts

   B. Show concern if someone is going through a difficult time

   C. To restate in his/her own words what another person has said

   D. Avoid asking a follow-up question when misunderstanding occurs.

2. Effectively demonstrate interpersonal skills means that the tourist guide will use their interpersonal skills in a perceptive manner.

   A. True

   B. False

3. Behavioral techniques for relieving stress include?

   A. Time management, positive thinking, reframing, ventilation and problem-solving

   B. Stretching exercise, breathing stretching exercise

   C. Taking a nap, watching T.V., listening to music

   D. Getting organized

4. We can experience multiple stressors arising from the demands of the different social roles we occupy, such as:

   A. Traffic, unsafe and substandard housing, and crime

   B. Deadlines, financial problems, job interviews, presentations, disagreements

   C. Illness, aging, giving birth, accidents, lack of exercise, poor nutrition, and sleep disturbances

   D. Weather, noise, crowding, pollution

5. To be effective you must modify the demands on your time. The approach to effective time management can be divided into 2 stages: identify values and set goals; develop mechanisms of effective time management.

   A. True

   B. False

Group Discussion

During the 2012 National Day holiday, Mr. and Mrs. Ma decided to travel to Maldives to celebrate their honeymoon. They paid 20 000 Yuan as travel fee for the package tour by the date mentioned in the contract document to China Dragon Travel Agency (CDTA) who is responsible for arranging the trip. Mrs. Huang, a tour leader from CDTA had been appointed the job to accompany the couples. When they arrived in Male, the capital of Maldives, they were received by a local tourist guide, Hassan.

Everything went wrong the following day. Hassan insisted that Ma couples had to pay 1 000 Yuan each to participate in diving; otherwise, the whole day's trip would be canceled. Mr. Ma tried to get Mrs. Huang for help, but Mrs. Huang only turned a blind eye to what had happen. As a result, Mr. Ma was forced to pay the extra fee for diving but felt very angry and he decided to write a complaint letter to the local tourism administration when they were back to Beijing.

1. Why the Ma couples decided to write a complaint letter to the local tourism administration?

2. What are the possible punishments that Mrs. Huang's inappropriate behavior would incur?

Guiding Exercise

Mr. Warren Buffett is chairman and CEO of Berkshire Hathaway and consistently ranked among the world's wealthiest people. He came to china to attend the World Expo Shanghai 2010.

When he was in Shanghai, you were his tourist guide accompanying him to visit Wuzhen, a 1 300 year old water town on the lower reaches of the Yangtze River. Mr. Jiang from Wuzhen Tourism Co. Ltd held a welcome banquet for Warren at a local restaurant. Warren expressed his interests in investing Wuzhen.

On the banquet, you were supposed to be the bridge to link the two sides together, as Warren can not speak in Chinese, nor did Mr. Jiang spoke in English.

Translation Exercise

1. Please translate the following passages into Chinese.

The Palace Museum, the world's largest existing and the most complete ancient building complex, is also a precious cultural heritage of mankind. There have been 24 emperors of the Ming and Qing Dynasties to govern and live here.

It currently has the world's largest and most complete preservation as well as the most exquisite built ancient buildings complex of palaces, with 1 500 000 books, historical relics and art treasures, and therefore gets the famous name of the Palace Museum.

The Palace Museum, historically and artistically one of the most comprehensive Chinese museums, was established on October 10, 1925 on the foundation of the palace that was the ritual center of two dynasties, the Ming and the Qing, and their collections of treasures. The collection of culture relics were mainly from the old stock of the palaces of the Qing Dynasty.

2. Please translate the following passages into English.

戏曲发源于初唐，在宋代快速发展。到元代，戏曲又称元杂剧，其又可分为短曲和杂剧。晚明时出现不少戏曲流派。清前期，又有倾向兼顾舞台效果的改革，及重视时事题材者。到了清乾隆末期，乾隆帝召全国戏班入京，其中又以"徽班"最闻名。至同治、光绪年间，发展出了"京剧"。

Case Study

Miss. Li has just passed the National Tourist Guide Accreditation Exam, and she is supposed to get her certificate of tour guiding in the coming February. She visited her friend, Mr. Tian, a tour operator working for the China Oriental Travel Company, and explained to him that she had strong passion for guiding career and asked for a chance to be a trainee tourist guide.

2 days later, she was appointed a job by him to send 10 Israeli tourists to the Beijing Capital International Airport. As scheduled, tourists were going to take Flight CA1485 to Chengdu at 5:00 pm; however, the airplane had been delayed for bad weather condition, they cannot leave until tomorrow morning at about 7:00 am. On that occasion, Miss. Li gave Mr. Tian a call to ask for help. Unfortunately, Tian did nothing but told her to keep calm. Li felt very helpless, and then she left all the tourists alone at the airport. As a result, her unprofessional reaction only caused complaints, and tourists all ask for compensation.

1. Please point out the impropriate conducts that this case has revealed.

2. Please discuss what should the company do in order to tackle the emergencies mainly caused by Miss Li and his Mr. Tian despite the poor weather condition?

Further Reading

A Concise History of China (2)

In 581 AD, a general named Yang Jian (entitled as Wendi after his death) from northwest China succeeded in conquering the other two kingdoms and establishing a new dynasty in China. This was the Sui Dynasty. Wendi decided to go back to the Han Dynasties' way of picking his government officials through universities and the great examinations; to find out who were the smartest and best-educated men.

Wendi's successor was his son, Yang Guang (Yang Ti), with his strong wishes for being a great emperor driving him, launched a lot of important projects. Yang Ti's best project was the Grand Canal which connected the Yellow River with the Huai and Yangtze Rivers and made it much easier to get from northern to southern China and back again.

Yang Ti, the last ruler of the Sui Dynasty, was killed in 618 AD by his generals, who blamed him for the disastrous defeat in the civil war. Li Shimin, a former high-rank official of Sui, took over ruling the empire, putting his father, Li Yuan, on the throne as emperor. By 626, Li Shimin made his father abdicate and took over the throne himself, historically known as Taizong. He made his capital at Chang'an, one of the biggest cities in the world at that time.

Taizong had a long reign and was a powerful emperor. He adopted the Han way of choosing governors and the Sui way of giving each man a grant of land and collecting taxes equally from everyone. He also took a census every three years to make sure that everyone paid the right amount of taxes. Under his rule, trade and cities became more important in China.

In 684 AD, after Taizong died, Wu Zetian became the regent for her young son. In 690, when she was 64 years old, Wu Zetian forced her son out and made herself Empress of China. As a devout Buddhist, she also promoted Taoism. She was a great ruler, and China was very successful both militarily and economically under her rule.

In 712 AD, Xuanzong became the new Tang emperor. Xuanzong was a great emperor who ruled a long time, and he succeeded greatly in expanding the borders of China.

But in the last years of his life, Xuanzong turned to art and philosophy, and lost interest in running his empire. In 755 AD, An Lushan led a rebellion against him. Xuanzong ran away to Sichuan. In 881 AD a revolt under Huang Chao ruined much of central China and destroyed the capital city-Chang'an. The Tang emperors had to move their capital eastward to Luoyang, where they never became powerful again.

The first part of the Song is called the Northern Song. In 960 AD, one general, named Zhao Kuangyin, managed to reunify central and southern lands of China. Zhao (historically known as Taizu) is known as a powerful emperor who kept the army firmly under his control. But his successors did not do as well, causing a weakened defense. The Song Dynasty never controlled an empire as large an empire as the Tang Empire had. In 1004 AD, the Song made peace with the Liao, and in 1044, they made peace with the Western Xia (or Xi Xia). The emperors had to pay gold to these people every year in order to keep the Liao in the north-east and the Xi Xia in the north-west from attacking. At about 1110 AD, the Song emperor made an alliance with the Juchens of Manchuria to fight the

Liao and get them out of northern China. But once the Liao was out, in 1115, the Juchens took over the Song capital of Kaifeng.

The second period of the Song is called the Southern Song. A prince of the Song ran away to southern China and in 1126 AD he started a new Song Dynasty with its capital at Hangzhou. The new Song Dynasty was not strong enough militarily, and could not take back the north from the Juchen, but they did develop a thriving trade. Because the Juchen had cut off their traditional route along the Silk Road, traders began sailing to south-east Asia and India. Bills helped to create growth in the economy. But in 1279 AD, the Mongols from north China came and killed the last of the Song emperors.

In 1276 the Mongols captured the Song capital at Hangzhou, and by 1279 the Mongols controlled all of China. Kublai Khan, the Mongol leader, moved its capital from Karakorum in Central Asia to Beijing. In 1271, when he was 56, Kublai Khan declared himself emperor of China.

Kublai Khan died in 1294 AD, and his successors were weaker and less able to keep the empire together. During the 1350's AD, a revolutionary movement called the Red Turbans became active in northern China. In 1356, the Red Turbans, under the leadership of Zhu Yuanzhang, captured Nanjing. Zhu Yuanzhang gradually conquered large parts of China. The Mongols were driven back to Mongol grasslands. In 1368 AD, Zhu Yuanzhang declared himself emperor of China, starting the Ming Dynasty.

After over-throwing the Yuan in 1368 AD, Zhu Yuanzhang established the Ming Dynasty. He modeled his government on the Tang Dynasty, trying to keep as much power as possible in the central government, especially in his own hands.

In 1451 AD, after a civil war, emperor Yongle moved the capital from Nanjing to Beijing, where he began work on the imperial palace or Forbidden City, which still stands today.

Like the Mongols in the 13th century, the Manchus (formerly the Juchen) succeeded in ruling the whole of China, but, unlike the 13th-century Mongols, the Manchus made their rule more acceptable to other Chinese. As a result, Qing's rule lasted 267 years, compared with 89 years of the Yuan. The Manchus took Beijing with relative ease in 1644, but they did not gain control of the whole China until 1683. Thereafter, the Manchus enjoyed more than a century of peace and prosperity, a period that came to be called Kangqian Shengshi (or, in a not so accurate term, Peace in China). By the end of that period the dynasty had reached its height of power.

The Revolution in 1911, the final years of the Qing resulted in the founding of the Republic of China. In the last years, foreign imperialism invaded China, causing a severe crisis for its survival and development. China witnessed many changes. After the May-Fourth Movement of 1919, the Communist Party of China was established and the Chinese revolution took on an entirely new appearance. In 1949, the People's Republic of China was founded and China entered a new phase.

Chapter 10
Group Management

Learning Outcome

After reading this chapter, you will be able to:

- Identify the types of group
- Know how to develop a group
- Understand the skills of poisoning the tour group
- Be aware of the teaching and learning strategies
- Understand how to avoid traveling risk
- Recognize how to manage conflicts with tour group

Opening Case

In December 20th, 2010, Mr. Tian, a local tourist guide from China Leisure Travel Agency, received 8 tourists from Macao. As scheduled, they would spend half day to visit both the Dufu's Thatched Cottage and the Wuhou Shrine; in the afternoon, they would take plane to Jiuzhaigou Valley.

For their visit to the Dufu's Thatched Cottage costs far more time than they expected, Mr. Tian is afraid that they would have not enough time to get to the airport in time, and he decided not to take the group to the Wuhou Shrine. Although his decision helped them saving time, he forgot to inform this to the tour leader and tour escort and got agreement from tourists. When they came back from Jiuzhaigou Valley, tourists complained and asked for refund.

1. Why the local tourist guide was complained by the tourists?
2. Should tourists' request for refund be supported?

Introduction

Tourist guides shall maintain a good working relationship with partners such as tour escorts and tour coach drivers, and the staff of all service providers such as tourist attractions, hotels, restaurants and tour coach companies, to ensure that the services specified in contracts are provided at the highest level. The purpose of this chapter is to discuss how to manage guiding group as well as tour group, particularly when facing risk and conflicts.

10.1 Group Types

Group can be defined as several individuals who come together to accomplish a particular task or goal. Group *dynamics* refers to the *attitudinal* and *behavioral* characteristics of a group, which concerns how groups form, their structure and process, and how they function.

There are many types of groups you may encounter in the workplace. One common way to classify group is by whether they are formal or informal in nature. Formal work groups are established by an organization to achieve organizational goals, including command groups, task groups, and functional groups.

Command Groups — command groups are specified by the organizational chart and often consist of a supervisor and the *subordinates* that report to that supervisor. An example of a command group is a manager in a travel agency and the faculty members in that company.

Task Groups — task groups consist of people who work together to achieve a common task. An example of *assigned* tasks is the tour service team, a temporary group and a task force. Members from travel and hospitality industry are brought together to accomplish goals of providing tourists with excellent services when travelling (Figure 10.1).

Functional Groups — a functional group is created by the organization to accomplish specific goals within an unspecified time frame. Examples of functional groups would be the tour guiding team (Figure 10.2).

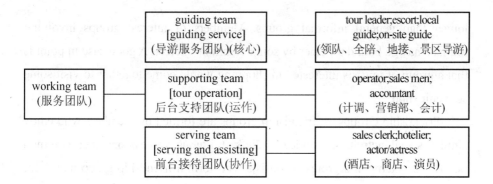

Figure 10.1 tour guiding team

Figure 10.2 Functional tour guiding group

In contrast to formal groups, informal groups are formed naturally and in response to the common interests and shared values of individuals. They are created for purposes other than the accomplishment of organizational goals and do not have a specified time frame.

Informal groups involving tourists are not appointed by any organization and members can invite others to join from time to time. The informal group of tourists can have a strong influence in tour service team. A group of tourists can take the form of interest groups, friendship groups, or reference groups.

Interest Groups — interest groups usually continue over time and may last longer than general informal groups. Members of interest groups involving tourists may be bound together by some common interest. A good case in point is that a group of tourists interested in shopping would come together to visit some souvenir shop.

Friendship Groups — friendship groups are formed by members who enjoy similar social activities, political beliefs, religious values, or other common bonds. For example, a group of tourists who form a friendship group may have an exercise group, a golfing team.

Reference Group — a reference group is a type of group that people use to evaluate themselves. Social *validation* allows individuals to *justify* their attitudes and values while social comparison helps individuals *evaluate* their own actions by comparing themselves to others. Reference groups have a strong influence on members' behaviors. By comparing themselves with other members, individuals are able to assess whether their behaviors are acceptable and whether their attitudes and values are right or wrong. Reference groups are different from the previously discussed groups because they may not actually meet or form voluntarily. For example, the reference group for a new employee of an organization may be a group of employees that work in a different department or even a different organization. Family, friends, and religious *affiliations* are strong reference groups for most individuals.

10.2 Group Development

When developing a group either tour working team or tourist group, it helps a great deal to have some basic sense of the stages that a typical team moves through when evolving into a high-performing team. Awareness of each stage helps tourist guide to understand the reasons for tourists behaviors and its counterpart during that stage, and to guide members to behaviors required to evolve the team into the next stage.

There are 5 stages of group development: forming, ***storming***, ***norming***, performing, and ***adjourning***. During these stages group members must address several issues and the way in which these issues are resolved determines whether the group will succeed in accomplishing its tasks, e.g. providing excellent guiding service.

Forming — members first get together during this stage. Individually, they are considering questions like, "What am I here for?", "Who else is here?" and "Whom am I comfortable with?" It is important for members to get involved with each other, including introducing themselves to each other. Clear and strong leadership is required from the team leader during this stage to ensure the group members feel the clarity and comfort required to evolve to the next stage.

Storming — during this stage, members are beginning to voice their individual differences, join with others who share the same beliefs, and jockey for position in the group. Therefore, it is important for members to continue to be highly involved with each other, including to voice any concerns in order to feel represented and understood. The team leader should help members to voice their views, and to achieve consensus (or commonality of views) about their purpose and priorities.

Norming — in this stage, members are beginning to share a common commitment to the purpose of the group, including to its overall goals and how each of the goals can be achieved. The team leader should focus on continuing to clarify the roles of each member, and a clear and workable structure and process for the group to achieve its goals.

Performing — in this stage, the team is working effectively and efficiently toward achieving its goals. During this stage, the style of leadership becomes more indirect as members take on stronger participation and involvement in the group process. Ideally, the style includes helping members to reflect on their experiences and to learn from them.

Closing and Celebration — at this stage, it is clear to members and their organization that the team has achieved its goals (or a major milestone along the way toward the goal). It is critical to acknowledge this point in the life of the team, lest members feel unfulfilled and *skeptical* about future team efforts.

In the early forming stage, the group is a collection of individuals, each with her/her own agenda and expertise and few or no shared experience. As these individuals become more familiar with one another, they will almost certainly enter a storming phase where personal values and principles are challenged, roles and responsibilities are taken on and/or rejected, and the group's objectives and way of working together are defined. At the norming stage, the group has settled down and developed a clear identity. The members have begun to understand their roles in relation to one another and establish a shared vision or goal. People know each other better; they have accepted the rules and probably developed little sub-groups. Once these norms have been established, the group will be ready to focus on output and will enter the performing phase. It is in this phase that they will work most effectively as a team. The confidence level of the team will have reached the point where they are willing to take significant risks and try out new ideas on their own.

10.3 Positioning of the Group

You are organizing a group of tourists, chatting with them, informing them about various places, partying with them, and sometimes even counseling them. You must be a leader. The following are tips for you to position your group and yourself as a tourist guide correctly during the Walking and Site Tours.

Choose position carefully — stand with your back to the object you are talking about but not directly in front of it so that it can be clearly seen; make use of natural windbreaks; be aware of the position of the sun or need for **shelter**; be aware of traffic noise.

Gather the group — gather the group around you; inform the group about where you are going.

Face the group — stand tall, do not slouch or lean on walls or vehicles; do not turn away from the group while talking; don't talk to the object; ensure that you can be heard.

Lead the group — lead the group to the area about which you intend to talk; avoid moving the group unnecessarily; avoid standing in cold or wet weather for a long time; be aware of the public and public access; be aware of the privacy of individuals and property; be mindful of the protection of the site e.g. use paths, do not touch objects.

Use open body language — do not fold arms; do not keep hands in pockets; control hand and arm gestures.

10.4 Risk Management

Travelling can be a very enlightening experience. Before **embarking** on such a journey, however, it is essential that we consider the possible risks associated with visiting a foreign country and take precautions in order to avoid or prepare for these risks. A stolen wallet or an unforeseeable illness could potentially ruin a long-awaited adventure and discourage any future possibilities.

Keep in mind that all trips must be given special consideration in terms of risk management as the nature of the visit, length of stay; destination and political and environmental conditions may have an impact on the severity and types of risks facing tourists. Tourist guide should encourage safety by the following tips below.

- Sit down in a moving coach;
- Inform group about safety, use of seat belts, first aid kit and emergency procedures;
- Give driver adequate warning of directions and be mindful of road conditions and traffic *restraints*;
- Be aware of driver's hours;
- Warn group of hazards e.g. while walking and on getting off the coach;
- Avoid using doors on offside of the coach unless in a safe area e.g. coach park;
- Choose safe routes and use crossings when walking;
- While walking control the group and keep them with you;
- Avoid walking backwards while talking.

10.5 Conflict Management

Conflict occurs with two or more people who, despite their first attempts at agreement, do not yet have agreement on a course of action, usually because their values, perspectives and opinions are *contradictory* in nature. Conflict can occur:

- Within yourself when you are not living in accordance to your values;

- When your values and perspectives are threatened;
- When there is discomfort from fear of the unknown or from lack of fulfillment.

Conflict is inevitable and often necessary when forming high-performing teams because they evolve through "form, storm, norm and perform" periods. Getting the most out of diversity often means addressing contradictory values, perspectives and opinions. Conflict is often needed. It:

- Helps to raise and address problems;
- Energizes work to be focused on the most important priorities;
- Helps people "be real" and motivates them to fully participate;
- Helps people learn how to recognize and benefit from their differences.

Conflict is not the same as discomfort. The conflict is not the problem — poor management of the conflict is the problem. Conflict is a problem when it:

- *Hampers* productivity;
- Lowers morale;
- Causes more and continued conflicts;
- Causes inappropriate behaviors.

Conflict is an inevitable part of working with groups of people who have different interests, backgrounds and experiences. Conflict need not be destructive if it is used constructively. Even small conflicts should not be ignored as they may grow out of proportion and affect the entire group. There is no *prescription* for dealing with group conflict. It will depend on the people involved, culturally bound ways of expressing dissent and disagreement, and your own style as a tourist guide.

It is important to get a sense of the nature of the conflict. It may simply be a function of the group life cycle. A storming phase may have little to do with course content or you as a trainer, and much more to do with group dynamics. It may be that individuals have hidden agendas outside the workshop theme that may conflict with declared group objectives. In group work, there are always trade-offs between individual and group objectives. Accepting such trade-offs can only happen if participants trust one another to agree on common objectives.

Conflicts between groups or individuals may be due to institutional affiliations, ideological or *political alliances*, religious or ethnic identification, professional relations or personality differences, about which you may know little. Raised voices, tense faces and nervous body language are all clear expressions of anger and conflict. Silence can also convey conflict, whether it is shown by the group, sub-group or an individual. While these symptoms may be relatively easy to observe, the root cause of the conflict may be harder to discover.

The following suggests some ways of reducing or reconciling conflicts that may arise during the trip.

- As soon as you see problems arise, take the opportunity to talk to the person individually. Sometimes *disruptive* people just want more individual attention.
- Do an activity, such as a "suggestion box", that allows complaints to be voiced and discussed *anonymously*.
- You can encourage participants to develop self-critical awareness about the quality and length of contributions to discussions.
- Only deal with difficult individuals publicly in exceptional circumstances.
- Reply to negative statements using positive terms such as "I respect ... and ..." or "I agree ... and ...". This tells tourists or your counterparts that you acknowledge and appreciate their perspective. You are showing that there is room for multiple opinions, and that each person's contribution is valued and encouraged.

Summary

Summary

This chapter is devoted to a discussion of group management, a key for successful tourist guide. Readers are expected to have elementary understanding of know-hows on group management, covering its type, development, positioning, risk management and conflict management.

Group in this chapter is subdivided into command group, task group, functional group, interest group, friendship group as well as reference group.

Group development is a process composed of 5 stages: forming, storming, norming, performing, closing and celebration.

Positioning of the group, it must be bear in mind, is of great significance for a tourist guide. It would be advisable for you to command key tips on choosing position, gathering, facing and leading the group, as well as using open body language.

All trips must given special consideration on risk management as the nature of the visit, length of stay; destination and political and environmental conditions may have an impact on the severity and types of risks facing tourists. Tourist guide must encourage safety through a number of useful tips.

A qualified tourist guide knows that conflict is not the problem, while poor management of the conflict is the real problem. He must manage destructive conflict in a timely, proper and advisable way.

Key Words and Phrases

Dynamic /daɪˈnæmɪk/ *noun*: the way that two or more people behave with each other because of a particular situation.

Attitudinal /ˌætɪtjuːdɪnəl/ *adjective*: relating to, based on, or showing a person's opinions and feelings.

Behavioral /bɪˈheɪvjərəl/ *adjective*: of the way a person or animal acts.

Subordinate /səˈbɔːdɪnət/ *noun*: someone who has less power or authority than someone else; someone who is subordinate to someone else.

Assign /əˈsaɪn/ *verb*: to give someone a particular job or duty, to require someone to complete a particular task.

Validation /ˌvælɪˈdeɪʃ(ə)n/ *noun*: to check the correctness of something.

Justify /ˈdʒʌstɪˌfaɪ/ *verb*: to provide or be a good reason for (something).

Evaluate /ɪˈvæljueɪt/ *verb*: to judge the value or condition of (someone or something) in a careful and thoughtful way.

Affiliation /əˌfɪliˈeɪʃ(ə)n/ *noun*: the state of belonging to a particular religious or political group.

Storming /ˈstɔːmɪŋ/ *noun*: here refers to a stage of goup development in which different ideas compete for consideration.

Norm /ˈnɔːm/ *verb*: to put sth into a standard, a model, or a pattern regarded as typical.

Adjourn /əˈdʒɜːn/ *verb*: to end something (such as a meeting or session) for a period of time.

Skeptical /ˈskeptɪkəl/ *adjective*: having or expressing doubt about something (such as a claim or statement).

Shelter /ˈʃeltə/ *noun*: a structure that covers or protects people or things.

Embark /ɪmˈbɑːk/ *verb*: to begin a journey especially on a ship or airplane.

Restraint /rɪˈstreɪnt/ *noun*: a way of limiting, controlling, or stopping something.

Contradictory /ˌkɔntrəˈdiktəri/ *adjective*: involving or having information that disagrees with other information; containing a contradiction.

Hamper /ˈhæmpə/ *verb*: to slow the movement, progress, or action of (someone or something).

Prescription /priˈskripʃ(ə)n/ *noun*: something that is suggested as a way to do something or to make something happen.

Alliance /əˈlaiəns/ *noun*: a group of people, countries, etc, that are joined together in some activity or effort.

Disruptive /disˈrʌptiv/ *adjective*: causing (something) to be unable to continue in the normal way.

Anonymously /əˈnɒːniməsli/ *adjective*: not named or identified.

Review Questions

1. How many processes are there for the group development?
2. How to successfully position a tour group?
3. What should be kept in mind in terms of risk management?
4. What should a tourist guide do in order to avoid travel risk?
5. How to manage conflicts within tour group?

Choice Questions

Choose the best answer to the questions below. You need to correctly answer 3 of the 5 questions to pass.

1. What types of group is this, if members from travel and hospitality industry are brought together to accomplish goals of providing tourists with excellent services when travelling would be regarded?

   A. Task groups

   B. Reference group

C. Functional group

D. Command group

2. When using open body language, what would you probably do?

A. Fold arms

B. Keep hands in pockets

C. Avoid eye contacts

D. Control hand and arm gestures

3. During the walking and site tours, what you should not do when positioning your group as tourist guide?

A. Stand with your back to the object you are talking about but not directly in front of it

B. Avoid standing in cold or wet weather for a long time

C. Lean on walls or vehicles when exhausted

D. Inform the group about where you are going

4. Tourist guide should encourage safety by not following one tip below?

A. Give driver adequate warning of directions and be mindful of road conditions and traffic restraints

B. Avoid using doors on offside of the coach unless in a safe area e.g. coach park

C. Choose safe routes and use crossings when walking

D. Walk backwards while talking

5. Which one is not the proper suggestion for reducing or reconciling conflicts that may arise during the trip?

A. Take the opportunity to talk to the disruptive people individually

B. Develop self-critical awareness about the quality and length of contributions to discussions

C. Reply to negative statements using terms such as "I think you are totally worry"

D. Only deal with difficult individuals publicly in exceptional circumstances

Group Discussion

According to the Beijing Tourism Administration, in the fourth quarter of 2008 Beijing received 20 complaints from tourists. These involved a total of 14 travel agencies. Out of the 20 complaints, 17 were about domestic travel. In particular, 11 of these were about the way Beijing received guests.

Most complaints were about the lack of service awareness and the poor sense of responsibility shown by some tourist guides in Beijing. In addition, they were also dissatisfied with travel agencies changing routes and supplying lower standards of accommodation and food. There were three complaints on outbound travel, which mainly involved trips to Thailand and Australia.

(Source: http://www.china.org.cn/travel/beijingguide/2009-01/09/content_17111374.htm.)

1. What are the main complaints?
2. How to improve service awareness and the poor sense of responsibility for tourist guides?

Guiding Exercise

After being with a group of 30 tourists from Hongkong SAR for 5 days, it is time to say goodbye. You are taking a shuttle bus from Royal hotel to the airport. You are supposed to deliver a memorable farewell speech. Obviously, it is always helpful to plan what you are going to say in advance. The following content will help you get your speech well prepared:

Farewell speech by tourist guide is to extend good wishes when tourists leave a place where they choose to stay for a short period of time. The main elements to have a successful and effective farewell speech are to convey a sense of regret at leaving and respect for people who have helped. The main elements of a farewell speech include:

- You should convey goodwill to all those who have been supportive and good wishes for the future;
- Your speech should also be short and remember to try to be humorous;
- Say some of your emotions when leaving.

The suggested outline of a farewell speech is as following:

- Your opener —the opening, ice-breaker or attention grabber;
- Main body — thank people for their support;
- The anecdotes — amusing stories and memories;
- Conclusion — extend your good wishes and try to end with a memorable or amusing farewell quote.

Translation Exercise

1. Please translate the following passages into Chinese.

Yungang Grottoes, a national key cultural relic protection unit, located in Datong City, Shanxi Province, has 252 grottoes and niches and more than 51 000 statues, representing the outstanding Chinese Buddhist grotto art from the 5 A.D. to 6 A.D. Tan Yao Cave, the most outstanding of all, well-structured and strictly-designed, is a classical masterpiece in the first peak period of the Chinese Buddhist art.

Yungang Grottoes have a history of more than 1 500 years, first built in 460 A.D., at the time begun by the Buddhist monk Tan Yao who built the grottoes under the emperor's order. The existing Yungang Grottoes groups are the first batch of national key cultural relic protection units declared by the State Council in 1961.

2. Please translate the following passages into English.

成都杜甫草堂博物馆是唐代诗人杜甫成都故宅旧址。杜甫草堂位于成都市区，是富有诗情画意和竹林风光的名园，为首批全国重点文物保护单位。

诗人杜甫于公元759年移居成都，历时3年9个月，在此作诗240余首，其名篇《茅屋为秋风所破歌》即居草堂之作。主要建筑有大廨、诗史堂、柴门、工部祠、少陵草堂等。草堂博物馆内珍藏各种历史资料3万余册，文物2 000余件，是研究"诗圣"杜甫的珍贵资料。

Case Study

In May 1, 2008, Mr. Stevenson and his 5 friends from Finland took part in a package tour to Tibet, and the trip was organized by Shanghai Paradise Travel Company. When they arrived at Lasa Gongga Airport, it was close to 11:00 pm. They were received by a local tourist guide, Zhaxi from Tibet Highland Travel Company.

Then he took the group to a Zhuoma restaurant to have lunch. After lunch, the group took tour bus to get to the hotel. As he helped the tourists check in, Stevenson felt stomachache and so did the rest people. Tourists were soon sent to the nearest hospital and found food poisoning. Though they all got recovered with 2 days intensive treatment, they were not able to finish the trip. As soon as coming back to Shanghai, they went to travel company in Shanghai and ask for refund and compensation.

1. Should tourists' request for refund and compensation be supported and why?
2. As a tourist guide, how to prevent food poisoning?

Further Reading

An Outline History of Ancient Chengdu

In the northern urban area of Chengdu city, a hill no more than 20 meters high solemnly stood. It used to be called Yangzi Shan. It was such an unnoticeable hill that 30 years ago a brick field was built nearby and the earth from the Yangzi Shan was used for brick production. This hill was to disappear gradually, until one day archeologists found that it was a man-made construction built thousands of years ago. The excavated remains proved that human beings had inhabited Sichuan Province as early as the latter Stone Age.

Around 4000—5000 years B.C., in the New Stone Age, people began to inhabit much larger areas. Their foot prints can be found in Chengdu, Xinjin, Chongzhou and other surrounding counties.

At approximately 1600—1100 B.C., a tribe that used to live in the upper reaches of the Minjiang River decided to migrate to the fertile Chengdu Plain. These people were a branch of the Qiang. The Qiang was one of the oldest nationalities in China. Led by Yufu, the earliest recorded king in Sichuan, they built houses above wetlands and made bronze out of tin and copper. They were not only simple hunters and gatherers but also farmers.

By the middle of the Western Zhou Dynasty, Yufu and his tribe gradually declined. Another tribe led by Duyu, still from the upper reaches of the Minjiang River, took over and a strong Kingdom appeared. Duyu himself was titled as King Wang (Wang Di), but there was one thing that threatened his monarchy. At that time, flood was the ruthless natural disaster tormenting the residences. It was said that a man named Bieling who came from the Chu Kingdom was an expert in fighting against flood. Duyu titled him the prime minister to conquer the merciless flood but later on, Duyu was forced to give his throne to Bieling, the great man who was more talented than him. After Duyu retired, Bieling, known as King Cong (Cong Di), led his people forward in the development of the kingdom and his successors ruled the ancient Shu Kingdom for about 500 years.

When the Shu people founded their kingdom in the western part of Sichuan, the Ba Nationality in the eastern part of Sichuan had founded another kingdom. The two neighbors were hostile to each other, for their hunger for lands and labors caused fierce wars. A prince of Shu was sent to defend Jiameng on the border and in secret; he colluded with the enemy state, making his brother, the king, mad. Thereafter, a war of revenge ignited forcing the prince in Jiameng to escape to the Ba Kingdom. In fact, the Ba kingdom was comparatively weaker. Naturally, the king of Ba had to ask for help from his powerful neighbor, the Qin Kingdom.

General Sima Cuo from the Qin believed that it was advisable to take advantage of this very chance to give the Ba Kingdom help in order to invade the two weaker states and to make Sichuan an important base for unifying the whole country. The aggressive king of Qin accepted his suggestion. It is in 316 B.C. that the powerful troops of the Qin climbed up the Mount Qin (Qing Ling) and went through the "Stone Bull Path" to enter Sichuan. It was not without resistance that finally the two were defeated.

After the ancient Shu Kingdom vanished from history, Chengdu became the capital of the Shu Prefecture belonging to the Qin. Zhang Ruo was authorized to be the first magistrate to the Prefecture. Since newly occupied, revolts abounded, therefore 3 grand cities named Chengdu, Pi and Lingqiong respectively were built in 310 B.C. for strengthening Qin's governing. Chengdu, as one of the three strong fortresses, was constructed with political and military urgency. With a wall 12 li (approximately 6 km) in length and 10 meters in height, Chengdu city was divided into Minor and Major Cities. This grand and magnificent city was built in the same style and size of Xianyang, the capital of the Qin Empire. It was said that the most difficult job was to build the wall because the fertile soil was too soft for any constructions to stand firmly. Fortunately, the city wall was successfully constructed upon a mysterious giant crawling tortoise, and left a nickname for Chengdu "the Tortoise City".

Dujiangyan Weirs was completed in 256 B.C.. Ever since then, this irrigation project has been in use on the Chengdu Plain. It is no doubt that the Dujiangyan Irrigation System is really a "symbol of Chinese civilization and the crystallization of the wisdom of ancient people". Beginning in 230 BC, 100 000 people from the northern part of the State of Qin moved to the Prefecture of Shu. They joined the local residents in developing the vast plain. Consequently, the prefecture became one of the largest grain granaries in the world, resulting in a rapid rise of the great power of Qin, the most powerful one in China then. In 223 B.C., The troops of Qin sailed from Chengdu by the Minjiang River into the Yangtze River and downstream to defeat the State of Chu. Two years later, China was reunified and Qin, the first unified feudal empire of China, was born.

During the last period of Jindi's reign in Western Han Dynasty, Wenweng was the magistrate to the Shu Prefecture. At that time, the economic development of Chengdu had reached a climax, but it was comparatively left behind culturally. Wenweng wanted to change this inequality through education.

Within a few years and with Wenweng's promotion, the local people's attitude to education had been greatly changed. More and more children were educated in the Stone House School and as a result, the quality of the education of the Shu Prefecture was vastly improved.

In the Western Han Dynasty, Chengdu was the center of the Shu Prefecture and in charge of 15 counties. Chengdu was the biggest city in the western region. Chengdu with a population of 350 000 was known as one of the five most flourishing cities, along with Luoyang, Linzi, Handan and Yuan, with the capital excluded from the account. Chengdu's local agricultural and handicraft products were well-known and highly sought after. As a result, administrations were set up to manage the production of carriage, brocade to name a few.

Thanks to Wenweng's promotion of education, Chengdu became a flourishing cultural center in the Western Han Dynasty, boasting a booming economy and having many talented scholars born in the Shu Prefecture. Sima Xiangru and Yang Xiong were the most prominent scholars among them.

Sima Xiangru, also named Changqing, was born in Chengdu. He was a true genius. Eloquence was not his strong point, but martial arts and literature were his favorites. The emperor appreciated his talents and ordered him to be his companion and stay with him. However, Sima Xiangru was not interested in that; instead he wanted to realize his talent of being a scholar.

After Sima came back to Chengdu, his hometown, he fell in love with a graceful lady named Zhuo Wenjun, a newly willowed musician. She bravely made the decision to get married with her beloved even against her parents' will.

Not long later, Sima Xiangru was appointed as a royal official. As a literati, he had written two persuasive essays to explain the importance of the emperor's policies. This proved to be a significant contribution to better the communication between the central government and the minority groups in the southwestern regions. During his life, he wrote many excellent works and was regarded as the best of his time. He died at the age of 63 and was highly praised in the Records of History.

Yang Xiong also named Ziyun was born in Pi County next to Chengdu. He lived in the last period of the Western Han Dynasty. Yang was a very hardworking student who read a lot of books. What made him outstanding was that he never turned a blind eye to mistakes that he found in the books. He was regarded as a linguist, literati, and philosopher. As a young man, Yang admired Sima Xiangru's literature talent and imitated his writing style. He had a similar opportunity to Sima to work as a companion for the emperor. He was ordered to write some flattering work. Then his talent was realized in the field of linguistics' and philosophical research. He wrote a book modeled after the Book of Changes and Fan Yan, which was an exposition of Confucianism modeled after the analects. A simple life at home accompanied his last years. For this great scholar, a fair comment is that no one could compare the achievements he made during his time.

The Origin of the Taoism

Taoism was born at about 2A.D.. Zhang Ling is known as the earlier founding father. Zhang was a native of Wu Prefecture in present day Zhejiang Province. He used to study in the capital and then in the hope of seeking a way to be immortal, he became a Taoist and started to spread Taoism.

In the year of 126A.D., Zhang came to the Hemin mount in Shu Prefecture and the beautiful scenery attracted him enough for him to stay. In his practice of spreading Taoism, he found that it was too costly for common people to believe in Taoism. Therefore, innovation was needed. What he did was to adopt the local people's beliefs and religions to localize Taoism. How to cure illness and to keep longevity was taught, to do the good, never the evil was the doctrine, and through these practices Taoism became popular. He honored Laozi as the Patriarch and his book Taotejin was the main doctrine, resulting in the birth of a more systematic Taoism. As his discipline requested, anyone who wanted to be his follower must donate some rice, hence the Taoism innovated by Zhang was also called "Rice Taoism". As the result of the wide spread of Taoism in Shu Prefecture, he divided the believing area into 24 sub-divisions. Today, the Green City Mount (Mt. Qingcheng) was once an important relic that he had been to spread his teachings.

The defeat of the Yellow Turban uprising at the end of the Eastern Han Dynasty was followed by a tangled warfare of more than ten years, between numbers of local feudal lords. That ended with the country being divided and ruled by the three of them. The Three Kingdoms period, in which the rival states of Wei, Shu and Wu existed side by side, dates approximately from 220 to 266AD.

Liu Bei was a not-so-powerful general. He had at his side the great statesman and military strategist Zhuge Liang and the services of the renowned generals Guan Yu, Zhang Fei and Zhao Yun. Claiming to be connected with the Han royal family, he was also preparing for a bid for power.

In 208A.D., Liu Bei joined forces with Sun Quan to defeat Cao Cao in the Chibi Battle. However, without a stable political base, Liu Bei had to bide his time by seeking the patronage of Liu Biao, the governor of Jingzhou.

In 221A.D., the governor of Jingzhou invited him to Sichuan. Liu Bei took this opportunity to lead his massive force to capture Yinzhou and soon, the vast land of Yinzhou was under Liu Bei's control. While Cao Pi proclaimed himself the Emperor of Wei in the north, Liu Bei in Chengdu declared himself the Emperor of Han, historically known as the Kingdom of Shu.

At the end of the Northern Zhou Dynasty, the rulership was in the hand of Yang Jian, a general, for the emperor was just a little kid. The general of the Shu Prefecture named Wang Qian led a revolt against Yang for his dictatorship. Therefore, Yang's powerful army soon marched to invade the Shu Prefecture.

In 581 A.D., Yang succeeded in conquering the other 2 kingdoms establishing a new Dynasty in China named Sui. What should be mentioned was that in the process of unification, Chengdu played an important role as a supplier of grains, weapons, and soldiers. After the founding of the Sui, the fourth son of Yang took the responsibility to govern the Shu Prefecture. During the restoration of the economy, Chengdu's population steadily increased to a large amount .For housing the increasing number of residents here, the governor of the Shu decided to enlarge the old city. According to the plan, the original outer city was enlarged for living while a Moha Lake was dug, which proved to be a wise solution for the amount of earth required to complete the outer city's construction was taken from the lake. The Moha Lake can be translated as "the Great Dragon Lake" and is said to next to the residence of the prince.

Yang Guang, the second and the last ruler of the Sui Dynasty, was killed in 618 A.D.. One of his generals, Li Yuan, was put onto the throne. By 626 A.D., he was forced to abdicate and his son, Li Shimin, became the emperor. It is under his regime that the capital, Chang'an, became one of the most prosperous and biggest cities in the world at that time.

During the Tang Dynasty, it was a house-hold word that Yangzhou was the most prosperous city while Chengdu was in the second place.

The Dujianyan irrigation system was repaired to promote the agriculture and Chengdu was noted not only for the production of wheat and rice but also for tea. The tea planted in Chengdu was sold throughout the country.

The long famed brocade industry in Chengdu was booming with the highly developed economy. Every year large amounts of brocades would be transported to the capital as taxes. The brocade produced in Chengdu from this time has even been found in Japan, which is proof that it was sold worldwide.

Chengdu was also a center for paper production. The high quality paper made in Chengdu gave impetus to the development of the Chinese writing culture. The famous Xue Tao's note was one of the best papers in Chengdu. Another famous product was the porcelain in Chengdu, featured for its colourful painting.

In Chengdu there were markets for brocade, silk, porcelain and many other local handicrafts, catering to the development of the economy.

A great many poets were born in the Tang Dynasty and their poems were to eulogize this prosperous era. What should be pointed out is that many of them were either natives of Chengdu or had a certain romance with Chengdu city. That all poets under heaven came to Chengdu was the slogan of that time and include Li Bai, Du Fu, and Xue Tao, to name just a few.

In the spring of 907A.D. Zhu Wen established the later Liang. Almost at the same time in the autumn of that year, the former Shu state was founded by Wang Jian, a garrison commander during the Tang Dynasty.

When Wang was young, he used to be a rouge then he joined the army to fight against the Huang Chao Revolt. His dedication and bravery to protect the emperor was soon noticed and appreciated. Wang took advantage of the chaos to rise up, caused by the peasant uprising, and was appointed as the governor of present day Sichuan. Later, he established the former Shu State as soon as the Tang Dynasty was toppled. Though Wang was not well-educated, he was fully aware of the importance of his talents. Wei Zhuang, a famed poet in the Tang Dynasty, was offered the responsibility to draft regulations and ordinances for the new kingdom. A talented lady pretending to be a man and traveling widely, but unfortunately was put into prison had been given an office to work for Wang.

Wang paid great attention to education and agriculture. He encouraged the establishment of new schools and the development of agriculture. The door of his kingdom was closed to avoid the negative influence of the fierce war in the central part of China at that time and under his rule, Chengdu became a prosperous and peaceful yet isolated land during the war time. After his death, his successor Wang Yan took the throne. In 925A.D., the former Shu was invaded and soon overturned due to bad ruling.

After the Former Shu was overthrown by the Later Tang, Chengdu was at war again, for the Later Tang State was not able to control the complicated political situation here. As a result, a general named Meng Zhixiang was sent to deal with the turmoil in Sichuan. With ambitious desire, Meng came to Chengdu. At that time, his biggest threat was Dong Zhang, a general, who occupied the eastern part of the Shu. For defending Dong, Meng ordered an earth wall commonly known as the Yangma Wall to be built around the old Chengdu city as a military defense.

In 932 A.D., Dong desired to establish his own state and came to challenge Meng. At the very beginning, it seemed that Meng was not able to defend the aggressive enemy troops. It was at the Mile Town that the situation was turned around in Meng's favour. Later, Dong was defeated and killed by his own followers.

The Later Tang deliberately appointed Meng the governor of the Shu for it was actually under his control. In 934A.D., the Later Shu was established by Meng who proclaimed himself emperor. But it was only a half year later that Meng was dead and his son, Meng Chang, crowned as the second ruler of the newly established kingdom. In fact, Meng Chang was not a bad ruler and in the earlier period of his regime, Chengdu recovered from the recession caused by war but unfortunately for the people of Shu, that peaceful life did not last long. It was said that Meng ordered the hibiscus to be planted on the Yangma Wall. When the hibiscus blossomed, the fragrance was carried 10's of miles away and accordingly, Chengdu city got another name the City of Hibiscus. Unfortunately, the Later Shu did not last long. In 965A.D., when the army of the Song Dynasty attacked Sichuan, Meng, the emperor, gave up defending, which paved the way for a new era.

In the last period of the Five Dynasties and Ten States, the living conditions of the peasants were at an all time low, which demanded a new era born. However, this painful situation was not changed at the beginning of the *Song Dynasty*.

In Sichuan, many farmers depended on tea production for survival under a government-controlled market. Many of them were unable to sustain their families and even themselves. Consequently, a great uprising broke out. Both Wang Xiaobo and Li Shun were tea farmers planting tea in the Green City Mount area where abundant tea plantations grew. In 993AD, a peasant uprisings led by Wang broke out. Wang was killed in the battle field and Li Shun, his brother-in-law, was given the responsibility to lead the uprising. The Dashu regime was established and Li was titled as the emperor after Chengdu was conquered in 994A.D.. The emperor of the Song was astonished by the uprising in Sichuan, and troops were sent to suppress it. After furious wars for several months, the Dashu was mercilessly erased, but the courage and heroic deeds of the Dashu soldiers will be remembered forever.

In 1234 A.D., after the collapse of the Jin Kingdom in northern China, Mongolians designed a plan to overthrow the declining Song, and occupying Sichuan was the first step. As the mounted troops began their march, the war could not be avoided. Yu Jie was ordered to fight against the Mongolian armies and he strategically constructed many strong fortresses. The fortress built on Yunding Mountain was 900 meters high, and was one of the strongest of its kinds in Sichuan. It was difficult for the Mongolians to conquer with its precipitous cliffs.

In 1252 A.D., a section of the Mongolian army marched to Jiadin in present day Leshan City. Failing to invade it, they went to camp at the foot of Yunding Mountain, 10 km away from the Jintang town. The Song soldiers made a surprise attack on the enemy camp at night and this was the first engagement in battle between the two. Two years later, the Mongolian armies were defeated again by the Song soldiers. In 1258A.D., the Song armies marching to Chengdu but were delayed by heavy rain and subsequently attacked on both wings. The desperate situation got worse. As they were in Yunding Mountain without aid and there were soon encircled by the Mongolian troops and consequently the fiercest war broke out. The battle lasted for several days but even after running out of ammunition and provisions, the soldiers refused to give up. With sticks and rocks, they continued to fight. At this critical moment, the Mongolian army broke through the defense line and seized the fortress making it the first time that Yunding Mountain was in the hands of Mongolians. In 1265A.D., the Song got a breakthrough in Jintang town. The next year, thirty thousand soldiers of the Song marched along the Tuo River to Guanghan. And with reinforcements from them, Song headed back to Yunding Mountain. Unfortunately Yunding Mountain was lost again, for the Song was too weak to overcome their enemies. It was more than 10 years that the war in Yunding Mount lasted. The heroic deeds that occurred during the resistance against the Mongolian army of that time would be remembered forever.

After the Southern Song was exterminated in 1276A.D., the Yuan Dynasty was founded. In the earlier years of the Yuan regime, Marco Polo, an Italian businessman, traveled through China. He followed his father and uncle in passing across the West and Central Asia and arrived at Shangdu in 1275A.D.. He was received by Kublai Khan, and welcomed by the emperor, and he was offered a position in the court.

He lived in China for 17 years and traveled around this marvelous land, which was a mystery to the westerners. One time, as an official, he traveled from Shanxi, to Sha'anxi and then, to Sichuan. When he arrived in Chengdu, he was deeply impressed by the prosperity and richness. When he sailed back to Venice, he described vividly the prosperity of Chengdu city in his book, Travels. It reads:

Chengdu, a grand and magnificent city, was located on a plain which covered an area of 32 square kilometers. There were many rivers running across it and some encircling the city. Those rivers ranging from 200 meters to 800 meters in width, originated from the mountains afar, providing plentiful water resources. There was a very huge bridge across the river in the downtown area. On the bridge was many houses built with wooden roofs, and supported by marble architecture. The tile-roofed corridors were painted with red pictures and used as a shelter in the rain. Along the bridge, those houses with many rooms and shops in line were in business (it is on the bridge) among which one was used as the administration office for taxation, offering the government a large amount of taxes from those wanting to cross.

Farmers lived outside the city while handicraft men lived within it, for a large amount of people made a living by handicrafts. They were good at silk and brocade making. The delicate silk and brocade made by them were extremely beautiful.

It was said that among the western travelers of this period none was better known than Marco Polo. Reportedly, His book *Travels* inspired such men as Christopher Columbus and Vasco da Gama in their search for a route to the east. And the book *Travels* is still a most valuable resource in studying the history of Chengdu.

In the center of downtown in present Chengdu City, there used to be numerous grand architectures. They were collectively called the "Forbidden City" by the Chengdu natives. In fact, those buildings were not the residence of the emperor; instead they were the former residence of the prince, the son of the emperor. As the Ming regime was newly established, in order to reinforce the control in Sichuan in the western region, one of his sons was sent to live in Chengdu. Before he came, a residence was designed and built for the prince. The construction work started in 1385A.D., and lasted about 5 years. If we took a bird's eye of the whole structure, we would find it shaped in a square with the main buildings standing along a central north-south axis (It does not exist any more).

For about 70 years, from the downfall of the Ming Dynasty to the earlier part of the Qing Dynasty, Sichuan had been shrouded in a dark cloud of war. Chengdu as its capital was the focus for those rebel armies struggling for power. After experiencing years of disaster caused by war, the population in Sichuan was greatly reduced. Take Chengdu as an example, the local residents were no more than 8 thousand then.

Without sufficient labor force, such a critical issue in Sichuan caused a decline in its development. So, the Qing government took great efforts to increase the population in Sichuan. Many policies were designed to encourage the residents in populated areas to migrate to Sichuan. Then a phenomenon popularly known as the migration from Huguang Province to Sichuan occurred. A great many migrants gave a great impetus to the development of Sichuan and their arrival brought far reaching influences to the local culture. This is the reason why Chengdu is a melting pot of multicultural.

Beginning in 1683 A.D., when it finally unified China, The Qing Regime took various measures to strengthen its rule. In military matters, the main force for fighting was the Manchu, Mongolian and Han Eight Banners. The soldiers of the Eight Banners were stationed across the country, from the nation's capital to small cities and towns. Chengdu as an important city in the western region was safeguarded by the Eight Banners' soldiers.

Based on the policy of enforcing the Manchu's statues, the Manchu's should live separately from the Han. Therefore, in 1718 A.D., a Manchu city was especially constructed for the Manchu's. It was also called Shaocheng or Small City, built to the west of the original city proper, with the length of about 4li (2 kilometers) and the height of 1zhang(about 3 meters). The magnificent Manchu city was also called Shaocheng or Small city. The city with five grand gates was in the shape of a fish. Standing along the north-south axis was Changshun Street which was in the middle of the city and 8 public streets were built on both sides for the Manchu's residents to live. The soldiers of the Eight Banners lived in some comparatively small streets and it was said that there were more than 20 thousand inhabitants. The streets were very flat lined with cypresses with tresses and decorated with flowers. The river called Jinhe ran across the city and the quality of life in the Manchu City was much better than the big city.

Appendix

Appendix Ⅰ Documentations for Oral Test of NTGAE

考生口试资格审核携带资料表

考生类别	携带物品
笔试合格考生 小语种考生	1. 口试准考证 2. 本人一寸红底免冠近照1张（照片应与报名信息一致） 3. 身份证（原件） 4. 学历证明（原件） 注：（1）在校大学生可出示学生证； 　　（2）国内学历证明遗失的，由毕业学校出具证明并加盖公章； 　　（3）持国（境）外学历学位的考生，需办理教育部留学服务中心《国（境）外学历学位认证书》，办理时间较长，请提前准备。 5. 健康证（原件，由县级及以上疾病预防与控制中心或防疫站出具的有效期内健康证）
加试考生	1. 口试准考证 2. 本人一寸红底免冠近照1张（照片应与报名信息一致） 3. 身份证（原件，复印件） 4. 导游员资格证书（原件，复印件） 5. 导游IC卡（原件）

Appendix Ⅱ Application Form for NTGAE

全国导游人员资格考试报名表（样表）

姓名		性别		民族	
身份证号					
报考语种	□中文　□英语　□日语　□德语　□法语　□泰语　□朝鲜语				
文化程度			所学专业		
中文资格证书号	（加试考生填写）		联系电话		
① 一寸 红底 免冠证件照		② 一寸 红底 免冠证件照		③ 一寸 红底 免冠证件照	
市（州）旅游局审核意见（盖章）　　　　　年　月　日					

注：报考语种只选填中文、英、日、德、法、泰、朝鲜语其中一种。

Appendix III Itinerary

	CHINA SUNSHINE TRAVEL AGENCY	
	ITINERARY OF SICHUAN PROVINCE	
	departure from home	
D1	taking off from the airport of Male to Chengdu city (around 6 hours).	Starway Jindi Hotel
D2	from airport to the hotel (within 1 hour by bus on condition of no traffic jam)	Starway Jindi Hotel
	picking up from the airport of Chengdu(about 7 am), heading for the hotel and having breakfast in the hotel. Free time for the group till dinner time, and dinner will be outside of the hotel. Lunch is not included today, you can have it in the hotel or outside of the hotel.	
D3	from Chengdu to E-meishan by bus	Jiataimei hotel

D3	After breakfast, leaving for Leshan Giant Buddha in the morning(120km, about 2.5 hours on condition of no jam), taking a break in a Crystal and Gem store for 45 minutes. Then heading for Leshan wharf(about 20 minutes). Having lunch near the wharf, then having a cruise in the Minjiang river for sightseeing the Leshan Giant Buddha(about 45 minutes). After the cruise, taking bus to E-mei shan mountain(about 45 minutes), dinner will be in the hotel today.	Jiataimei hotel

D4	from E-mei shan to Chengdu City by bus	Starway Jindi Hotel
	After breakfast, leaving for Baoguo temple(about 30 minutes from the hotel),the bus will stop in the Baoguosi parking lot. Walking 8 minutes to Baoguo temple, spend 40 minutes there. Then walking to the Fuhu temple(about 30 minutes), spend 45 minutes in the temple. Then walking back to the parking lot for lunch. After lunch heading for Big Buddha temple by bus(about 20 minutes), spending 50 minutes there. Heading back to Chengdu City for dinner(about 2.5 hours on condition of no jam), after dinner back to hotel.	

D5	sightseeing in Chengdu city	Starway Jindi Hotel
	After breakfast, heading for Qingtai street(25minutes by bus), this is ancient street for memorialize a famous local poet and his wife. Spending 50 minutes there, then taking bus to Kuanzhai alley, spending 1hour in the alley. Then heading for restaurant by bus, after	

D5	lunch visit the silk factory which is the intangible heritage issued by our government, spending 50 minutes there. Then taking bus to Jingli ancient street, spending 1hour there. After the ancient street ,taking bus to restaurant for dinner and back to hotel.	Starway Jindi Hotel
D6	shopping in Chengdu City After breakfast, heading for Suning household appliance store by bus(about 30 minute), Suning appliance store is one of the China's top dealer which is very good at the sales of electronic household appliance! The group will stay there until lunch time. Taking bus to the restaurant for lunch. After lunch, heading for Tibet medicine shop for foot massage. After that, taking bus to clothes exhibition building at new century Chengdu convention center for sightseeing. Then going to the restaurant for dinner and back to the hotel,	Starway Jindi Hotel
D7	shopping in Chengdu City	Starway Jindi Hotel
D8	taking plane to Male Breakfast will be in the hotel, but lunch and dinner are not covered by travel agency. Preparing your luggage before 12 o'clock and storing in the hotel, free time in the city. Leaving from the hotel to airport at 6o'clock.	

Appendix Ⅳ Schedule

旅行社团队运行计划表　00000005022

团名	CNTJ20120720	人数	2	组团社	中国阳光国际旅行社	全陪	张一
抵离时间	7月 20 日 8 时 00 分 由 北京 乘 8888 航班/车次抵成都					地陪	刘二
	第一次 7月 26 日 11 时 00 分 由 成都 乘 8887 航班/车次抵北京					驾驶员	张三
	第二次 　月　日　时　分 由　　分乘　航班/车次抵					车型	金杯
						车号	川 A111

行程安排	早餐地点	游览景点及时间	午餐地点	午餐标准	游览景点及时间	晚餐地点	购物点	自费项目	住宿酒店
7月 20 日		接机成都至乐山	乐山	20元/人	乐山大佛	峨眉山	水晶	东方佛都	峨眉山温泉酒店
7月 21 日	酒店	峨眉山景区	峨眉山景区	20元/人	峨眉山至成都	成都	无	无	成都皇冠假日酒店
7月 22 日	酒店	成都至都江堰	川主寺	20元/人	九寨沟	九寨沟	无	烤羊	九寨喜来登酒店
7月 23 日	酒店	九寨沟景区	诺日郎餐厅	50元/人	九寨沟景区	酒店	无	晚会	九寨喜来登酒店
7月 24 日	酒店	九寨沟至川主寺	川主寺	20元/人	黄龙景区	川主寺	水晶	无	川主寺岷江源酒店
7月 25 日	酒店	川主寺至茂县	茂县	20元/人	茂县至成都	成都	无	无	成都皇冠假日酒店
7月 26 日	酒店	送机							
备注	游客自主决定是否参加自费项目								

旅行社投诉电话　028-8660000　各级旅执法（质监）机构投诉电话 （区号）+9627

旅行社公章　　　　　　　　　　　　　　　　　　　　　　　四川省旅游执法总队印制

Appendix Ⅴ Name list

Bus	Room	Title	First-name	Last-name	Passport No.	Date of Birth	Date of Issue	Date of Expiry
Bus 1	1	Mr.			C60000	1980/×/×	2005/×/×	2010/8/1
Bus 1	1	Master			K62000	1999/×/×	2005/×/×	2010/12/29
Bus 1	1	Mrs.			V50300	1957/×/×	2004/×/×	2009/9/28
Bus 1	2	Mrs.			W59800	1959/×/×	2005/×/×	2010/2/28
Bus 1	2	Miss			K63200	1999/×/×	2006/×/×	2011/1/15
Bus 1	3	Miss			P662300	1980/×/×	2006/×/×	2011/5/7
Bus 1	3	Miss			R706100	1957/×/×	2008/×/×	2013/2/1
Bus 1	4	Mrs.			K626200	1966/×/×	2006/×/×	2011/1/8
Bus 1	4	Mr.			Z622600	1982/×/×	2007/×/×	2012/1/16
Bus 1	5	Miss			A870000	1965/×/×	2009/×/×	2014/1/8
Bus 2	23	Miss			I699000	1978/×/×	2005/×/×	2010/12/21
Bus 2	23	Miss			V571000	1987/×/×	2004/×/×	2009/12/22
Bus 2	24	Mrs.			L733000	1957/×/×	2007/×/×	2012/12/26
Bus 2	24	Mrs.			S775000	1959/×/×	2008/×/×	2013/6/23
Bus 2	25	Mrs.			B88000	1953/×/×	2009/×/×	2014/1/25
Bus 2	25	Mr.			B883000	1965/×/×	2009/×/×	2014/1/25
Bus 2	26	Mr.			L746000	1963/×/×	2008/×/×	2013/1/22
Bus 2	26	Mrs.			L746000	1967/×/×	2008/×/×	2013/1/22
Bus 2	27	Mrs.			W603000	1965/×/×	2006/×/×	2011/10/12
Bus 2	27	Miss			G744000	1978/×/×	2007/×/×	2012/6/3
Bus 2	28	Miss			B861000	1929/×/×	2009/×/×	2014/1/29

Appendix VI Questionnaire for guiding service

旅行社服务质量跟踪调查表

团名			人数		全陪	
地陪		车号			驾驶员	
游客意见	非常满意		满意	基本满意	不满意	
日常安排						
导游服务						
餐饮质量						
娱乐项目						
交通保障						
购物安排						
旅游安全						
其他						
备注	（1）为了切实保护游客的合法权益，加强对旅游经营者特别是导游人员的监督管理，特制定本表。 （2）团队抵达时。由导游将本表分发给每位游客。 （3）导游不得随意更改团队运行计划。 （4）导游不得向游客索要小费。 （5）游客如对表中所列项目不满意，可向各级旅游执法（质监）投诉。投诉电话：96927 投诉地址：　　　　　　　　　　邮政编码：						

四川省旅游局监制
四川省旅游执法总队印制

Appendix Ⅶ Insurance

中国人民财产保险有限公司

2010版旅游意外伤害保险投保清单（暨承保确认书）

旅行社	中国阳光旅行社	导游	张×	旅行时间	2011年8月26日 时起至 2011年8月29日 时止		
团队号	20110826B	经办人	李×				
旅行路线	九黄双汽4天	旅行人数	人	联系电话		传真	
旅游形式	常规□ 自驾游□ 自由人□			是否有高风险旅游项目	有□ 无□		
序号	姓名	身份证号码/护照号码	国籍	序号	姓名	身份证号码/护照号码	国籍
1	高×	512222196507000000	中国	14			
2	苏×	652322196311000000	中国	15			
3	苏×	652322199212000000	中国	16			
4	张×	652322196406000000	中国	17			
5	潘×	412921195809000000	中国	18			
6	尹×	411326198704000000	中国	19			
7	王×	411326198504000000	中国	20			
8	潘×	411326199202000000	中国	21			
9	明×	510221196001000000	中国	22			
10	何×	650300196805000000	中国	23			
11	刘×	650300196901000000	中国	24			
12	唐×	512222196704000000	中国	25			
13				26			
备注	1. 常规团承保范围是指：在旅行社导游的陪同下乘坐合法有旅游资质的交通工具，按照旅游合同中约定的时间、路线的行程。 2. 特殊旅游或者高风险指：被保险人在旅游景区内参加非职业性、非竞技性带有娱乐性的赛车、赛马、登山、滑翔、漂流、探险、潜水、滑草、滑沙、滑板、冲浪、跳伞、热气球、蹦极等具有高风险的旅游活动。 自由人的承保范围是指：保险人只承担游客与旅行社签订的代订合同中明确了的在交通工具上发生的和酒店/宾馆内发生的意外事故，其他意外事故不在保险责任范围内。 3. 旅游意外保险时间是指：当游客按照旅游合同登上由旅行社安排的有合法资质的交通工具（如火车、汽车、飞机、轮船等）开始，直至游客行程结束离开旅行社安排的合法资质交通工具结束。 4. 旅行社负有向被保险人如实告知保险责任、责任免除、保险期间、赔付标准及赔付比例等相关内容的义务，旅行社同时负有向我公司如实告知的被保险人相关情况的义务，我公司承保内容以收到传真清单为准。 5. 保险金额和责任、责任免除、保险期间、赔付标准等参照旅行社与我公司签订的旅游意外险协议的具体规定。 6. 在旅游形式中未注明的按常规团承保，在高风险旅游项目中未注明的按无高风险承保。						
内宾人数 人，旅游天数 天 外宾人数 人				内宾人数 人，旅游天数 天 外宾人数 人			
旅行社确认人： 签字盖章： 年 月 日				保险公司确认人： 签字盖章： 年 月 日			
保险公司传真： 电话：							

Appendix VIII Expense Account

中国阳光旅行社欧美部团队报销单

团号:		人数:		导游:		司机:		报销日期:	
天数	日期	中餐	晚餐	房费		门票		杂费	
D1								地司:	
D2								行李车:	
D3								杂技:	
D4								机票:	
D5								车费:	
D6									
D7									
D8									
小计									
合计		现金:				签单:			
总计		借款金额:		应退金额:				应补金额:	
S/P	店名								
	人数								
	金额					单团毛利:			
	财务								
应收财款:									

参 考 文 献

[1] 陆志宝. 导游英语[M]. 北京：旅游教育出版社，2005.
[2] 国家旅游局人事劳动教育司. 中级导游员系列丛书：英语[M]. 北京：中国旅游出版社，2004.
[3] 朱歧新. 英语导游翻译实用手册[M]. 北京：旅游教育出版社，1995.
[4] 朱华，等. 四川英语导游景点讲解[M]. 北京：中国旅游出版社，2004.
[5] 杨天庆. 四川导游英语应试必备手册. 成都：四川科学技术出版社，2002.
[6] 段开成. 旅游英语(高级) [M]. 天津：南开大学出版社，1998.
[7] 熊剑平，李志飞，张贞冰. 导游学：理论·方法·实践[M]，北京：科学出版社，2007.
[8] 刘洪利. 导游学[M]. 北京：清华大学出版社有限公司，2008.
[9] 陈建勤. 新编导游学概论[M]. 太原：山西教育出版社，2007.
[10] 吕宛青，仇学琴. 旅游导游学[M]. 昆明：云南大学出版社，1994.
[11] 陶汉军，黄松山. 导游服务学概论[M]. 北京：中国旅游出版社，2003.
[12] 赵爱华. 导游概论[M]. 北京：中国旅游出版社，2009.
[13] 姚宝荣. 模拟导游教程(修订版)[M]. 北京：中国旅游出版社，2004.
[14] 赵明. 导游业务知识(最新版)[M]. 昆明：云南大学出版社，2007.
[15] 生延超，范保宁. 导游理论与实务[M]. 北京：中国旅游出版社，2007.
[16] 后智钢. 导游业务[M]. 福州：福建人民出版社，2007.
[17] 龚维嘉. 导游业务[M]. 合肥：合肥工业大学出版社，2008.
[18] 李兴荣. 模拟现场导游[M]. 成都：四川大学出版社，2008.
[19] 叶骁军. 导游技能实务[M]. 天津：南开大学出版社，2008.
[20] 赵湘军. 导游学原理与实践[M]. 长沙：湖南人民出版社，2003.
[21] 陈永发. 导游学概论[M]. 上海：上海三联书店，2000.
[22] 张建融. 导游服务实务[M]. 杭州：浙江大学出版社，2005.
[23] 姜福金. 导游实务[M]. 大连：大连理工大学出版社，2006.
[24] 魏芬. 导游业务[M]. 北京：中国物资出版社，2007.
[25] 谢攀峰. 导游与旅行社业务[M]. 北京：科学出版社，2007.
[26] 浙江省旅游局. 导游业务[M]. 北京：中国旅游出版社，2007.
[27] 袁俊，夏绍兵. 导游业务[M]. 武汉：武汉大学出版社，2008.
[28] 冯云艳. 导游业务实务教程[M]. 北京：中国纺织出版社，2009.
[29] 樊丽丽. 导游业务训练课程[M]. 北京：中国经济出版社，2007.
[30] 国家旅游局人事劳动教育司. 导游业务[M]. 4版. 北京：旅游教育出版社，2004.
[31] 马伯健. 导游业务[M]. 4版. 大连：东北财经大学出版社，2008.
[32] 李亚妮. 导游业务[M]. 北京：清华大学出版社有限公司，2009.
[33] 陶汉军，黄松山. 导游业务[M]. 天津：南开大学出版社，2005.
[34] 李红，覃楚艳. 导游业务[M]. 武汉：华中科技大学出版社，2008.
[35] 刘国强，张辉. 导游业务实训教程[M]. 北京：科学出版社，2008.

[36] 蒲阳. 导游业务[M]. 北京：机械工业出版社，2009.
[37] 胡晓勤. 导游业务实训教程[M]. 北京：科学出版社，2008.
[38] 熊剑平，袁俊. 导游业务[M]. 武汉：武汉大学出版社，2004.
[39] 陈乾康. 导游实务[M]. 北京：中国人民大学出版社，2006.
[40] 江定祥. 全国导游人员资格考试模拟金题：导游业务[M]. 武汉：华中科技大学出版社，2010.
[41] 王昆欣. 全国导游人员资格考试模拟试题汇编[M]. 3版. 北京：旅游教育出版社，2009.
[42] 鲍文君. 导游原理与实务[M]. 北京：电子工业出版社，2009.
[43] 侯志强. 导游服务实训教程[M]. 福州：福建人民出版社，2003.
[44] 徐堃耿. 导游概论[M]. 4版. 北京：旅游教育出版社，2008.
[45] 方海川. 导游原理与实务[M]. 成都：西南财经大学出版社，2009.
[46] 冯霞敏. 导游实务[M]. 上海：上海财经大学出版社，2008.
[47] 林梅英. 导游实务[M]. 郑州：郑州大学出版社，2006.
[48] 陈瑜. 导游服务技能[M]. 北京：机械工业出版社，2008.
[49] 杜炜，张建梅. 导游业务[M]. 2版. 北京：高等教育出版社，2006.
[50] 郭书兰. 导游原理与实务[M]. 3版. 大连：东北财经大学出版社，2006.
[51] 周彩屏. 模拟导游实训：任务驱动型[M]. 北京：中国劳动社会保障出版社，2008.
[52] 李瑞玲. 导游业务[M]. 郑州：郑州大学出版社，2006.
[53] 唐德鹏. 导游业务[M]. 福州：福建人民出版社，2005.
[54] 全国导游人员资格考试教材编写组. 导游实务[M]. 北京：旅游教育出版社，2008.
[55] 赵阳. 导游实务[M]. 哈尔滨：哈尔滨工业大学出版社，2005.
[56] 叶华胜. 导游业务[M]. 北京：人民邮电出版社，2006.
[57] 吕莉. 导游业务[M]. 北京：中国商业出版社，2005.
[58] 浙江省旅游局. 导游业务[M]. 北京：中国旅游出版社，2004.
[59] 黄明亮，刘德兵. 导游业务实训教程[M]. 北京：科学出版社，2007.
[60] 问建军. 导游业务[M]. 北京：科学出版社，2005.
[61] 杨光，王冬青. 导游业务[M]. 北京：电子工业出版社，2007.
[62] 窦志萍，岳怀. 模拟导游[M]. 北京：高等教育出版社，2007.
[63] 虞国华. 导游服务管[M]. 广州：广东旅游出版社，2001.
[64] 陈临蓉. 导游实务[M]. 成都：西南财经大学出版社，2006.
[65] 易伟新，刘娟. 导游实务[M]. 北京：清华大学出版社，2009.
[66] 朱歧新，张秀桂. 英语导游翻译必读[M]. 北京：中国旅游出版社，1999.
[67] 黄俊武，李飞. 导游薪酬问题的产生根源及其治理措施[J]. 特区经济，2007(6).
[68] 秦楠. 浅析文化型导游及其对旅游业的影响[J]. 黑龙江对外经贸，2009(6).
[69] 刘启亮. 诚信旅游与导游管理[J]. 承德职业学院学报，2006(2).
[70] 贵琳. 文化的传播——导游翻译[J]. 群文天地，2012(2).
[71] 刘桂村. 游客"对导游的评价"情况调查结果与分析——以四川省成都地区为例[J]. 湖北经济学院学报(人文社会科学版)，2012(7).

[72] 敬丽丽，李晓东，邓方江. 导游工作满意度影响因素的排序研究[J]. 中国管理信息化，2009(4).

[73] 许丽君，江可申. 基于收益分享理论的导游激励机制设计[J]. 统计与决策，2008(12).

[74] 高源. 论工作投入与避免导游工作倦怠[J]. 现代商贸工业，2012(5).

[75] 洪磊. 在实践性教学中探索导游核心能力的培养[J]. 网络财富，2010(11).

[76] 黄妩. 浅谈导游的心理压力与心理调适[J]. 法制与经济(下旬)，2010(9).

[77] 杨奇美，郑弋炜，任福来. 工作任务为导向的现场教学模式的实践与研究——以导游专业实践教学为例[J]. 赤峰学院学报(自然科学版)，2009(6).

[78] 田喜洲，田敏. 旅行社与导游委托代理模型解析[J]. 旅游学刊，2009(6).

[79] 赵宇. 北京导游资格证考试基础知识教与学探析[J]. 价值工程，2011(26).

[80] 王玉琼，贾贵洲. 教育智慧视域下的导游培养[J]. 江西科技师范学院学报，2010(2).

[81] 杨梅. 关于英语导游非语言交际行为和手段的研究[J]. 旅游学刊，2005(S1).

[82] 田喜洲，蒲勇健. 导游工作满意度分析与实证测评[J]. 旅游学刊，2006(6).

[83] 梁唯. 互动式教学法在导游实务教学中的应用[J]. 中小企业管理与科技(上旬刊)，2009(10).

[84] 王淑娟. 导游队伍可持续发展的路径[J]. 改革与开放，2010(18).

[85] 杨辉强，王野，韦福巍. 浅谈《导游实务》课程教学改革——以河池学院旅游管理专业为例[J]. 大众文艺，2011(18).

[86] 杨健，王怡然. 我国导游诚信问题浅析[J]. 特区经济，2007(6).

[87] 杨慧. 导游翻译中普遍存在的问题及解决途径探析[J]. 双语学习，2007(12).

[88] 刘春济，高静. 国内旅游者对国内导游服务质量的评价研究[J]. 北京第二外国语学院学报，2006(9).

[89] 罗文标. 涉外导游培养模式探讨[J]. 现代交际，2010(4).

[90] 罗春科. 《导游业务》课程教学初探[J]. 科技信息(科学教研)，2007(26).

[91] 李萌，何春萍. 论导游在旅游地形象建设中的作用[J]. 国际商务研究，2002(2).

[92] 刘纯. 论导游的心理品质及其对旅游者行为的影响[J]. 社会科学家，1988(1).

[93] 孟冬玲. 《导游基础》课教学初探[J]. 职业教育研究，2004(3).

[94] 余志远，周广鹏. 导游：一类非制度性生存状态中的矛盾主体[J]. 北京第二外国语学院学报，2011(3).

[95] 程立初. 导游专门用途英语多媒体教学经验浅谈[J]. 北京第二外国语学院学报，2006(6).

[96] 刘春济，高静. 国内旅游者对国内导游服务质量的评价研究[J]. 北京第二外国语学院学报，2006(9).

[97] 王湘. 浅议导游资格考试辅导教材的质量监控——以《导游人员资格考试指定教材》为例[J]. 北京第二外国语学院学报，2003(5).

[98] 林刚，宋延巍. 导游人员道德风险行为分析[J]. 北京第二外国语学院学报，2004(1).

[99] 刘爱服. 英语导游课程的特征及教学探讨[J]. 北京第二外国语学院学报，2004(6).

[100] 姜彩芬，曾文标. 谈提高旅行社导游员管理中的公平性[J]. 北京第二外国语学院学报，2002(1).

[101] 钱炜. 中国旅游教育与培训：进步、问题和对策[J]. 北京第二外国语学院学报，1994(3).

[102] 陈永昶，徐虹，郭净. 导游与游客交互质量对游客感知的影响——以游客感知风险作为中介变量的模型[J]. 旅游学刊，2011(8).

[103] 宋一兵. 大学生导游职业认知形成及其改善[J]. 旅游学刊，2012(10).

[104] 田喜洲，田敏. 旅行社与导游委托代理模型解析[J]. 旅游学刊，2009(6).

[105] 田喜洲，蒲勇健. 导游工作满意度分析与实证测评[J]. 旅游学刊，2006(6).

[106] 杨梅. 关于英语导游非语言交际行为和手段的研究[J]. 旅游学刊，2005(S1).

[107] 孙圣英. 旅游法语笔译和导游课的"和而不同"[J]. 旅游学刊，2005(S1).

[108] 魏咏梅.《导游业务》课程教改总结[J]. 旅游学刊，1998(S1).

[109] 张莹. 导游资格考试制度存在问题及对策分析[J]. 经济研究导刊，2010(12).

[110] 王湘. 浅议导游资格考试辅导教材的质量监控——以《导游人员资格考试指定教材》为例[J]. 北京第二外国语学院学报，2003(5).

[111] 杨智勇. 现行导游资格考试制度存在问题及取消的尝试[J]. 内蒙古科技与经济，2009(14).

[112] 李雯，杨志勇. 现行导游资格考试制度存在的问题及思考[J]. 内蒙古财经学院学报(综合版)，2009(2).

[113] 袁尧清，方磊，唐德彪. 从导游资格考试谈导游人员史地知识能力的培养[J]. 商业经济，2009(2).

[114] 王芳. 基于"学习型导游"培养的"导游资格考试系列课程网络试题库和自测/考评系统"的构建[J]. 中国校外教育，2010(S1).

[115] 刘是今. 导游资格考试制度的重新审视[J]. 湖南第一师范学报，2008(1).

[116] 刘春梅. 中外导游管理制度的比较研究[J]. 商场现代化，2007(19).

[117] 沈民权.《导游文化基础知识》课程的定位、特点与教学建议[J]. 职业，2011(27).

[118] 李平. 导游人力资源现状及开发管理对策[J]. 经济工作导刊，2003(20).

[119] 张丹宇. 日本的导游管理制度[J]. 重庆与世界，1999(5).

[120] 吕珊珊.《导游业务》教学改革刍议[J]. 吉林工程技术师范学院学报，2007(5).

[121] Verite Reily Collins. Becoming a tour guide: the principle of guiding and site interpretation[M]. London: Thomson Learning, 2000.

[122] Cruz Z. Principles and ethics of tour guiding[M]. Manila: Rex Printing Company, 1999.

[123] Trevor Waller, Debbie Nafte. Tour guide[M]. Gallo Manor: Awareness Publishing House, 2007.

[124] Ginger Todd, Susan Rice. A guide to becoming a travel professional[M]. New York: Thomson Delmar Learning, 2005.

[125] Marc Mancini. Conducting Tours[M]. New York: Thomson Delmar Learning, 2001.

[126] Bruce Prideaux, Gianna Moscardo, Eric Laws. Managing tourism and hospitality services: theory and international applications[M]. London: CAB International, 2006.

[127] Kathleen Lingle Pond. The professional guide: dynamics of tour guiding[M]. New York: John Wiley & Sons Inc., 1992.

[128] Verite Reily Collins. Working in tourism: the uk, europe & beyond for seasonal and permanent staff [M]. London: Crimson Publishing, Limited, 2004.

[129] Cherie Turner. Adventure Tour Guides: Life on Extreme Outdoor Adventures[M]. New York: Rosen Publishing Group, 2003.

[130] Barbara Braidwood, Richard Cropp, Susan M. Boyce. Start and run a profitable tour guiding business:part-time, full-time, at home, or abroad[M]. Bellingham: Self-Counsel Press, Nov, 2000.

[131] Alison L. Grinder, E. Sue McCoy Grinder, Alison L. The good guide: a sourcebook for interpreters, docents, and tour guides[M]. Florida: Ironwood Publishing,1985.

[132] Barbara Abramoff Levy, Sandra Mackenzie Lloyd, Susan Porter Schreiber. Great Tours: Thematic Tours and Guide Training for Historic Sites[M]. Lanham: Altamira Press, 2002.

[133] Ap J, Wong K K F. Case study on tour guiding: professionalism, issues and problems. Tourism Management. 2001, 22(5).

[134] Bryon. J. Tour guides as storytellers — from selling to sharing. Scandinavian Journal of Hospitality and Tourism, 2012, 12(1).

[135] Buzinde C, Choi Y, Wang A Y. Tourism representations of Chinese cosmology: the case of feng shui tourism. Annals of Tourism Research. 2012, 39(2).

[136] Chang R C Y, Kivela J, Mak A H N. Attributes that influence the evaluation of travel dining experience: When East meets West. Tourism Management. 2011, 32(2).

[137] Cohen E. The tourist guide — the origins, structure and dynamics of a role. Annals of Tourism Research. 1985(12).

[138] Cole S. Implementing and evaluating a code of conduct for visitors. Tourism Management. 2007, 28(2).

[139] Dahles, H. The politics of tour guiding - image management in indonesia. Annals of Tourism Research. 2002, 29(3).

[140] Fine E C, Speer J H. Tour guide performances as sight sacralization. Annals of Tourism Research. 1985(12).

[141] Gelbman A, Maoz D. Island of peace or island of war: tourist guiding. Annals of Tourism Research. 2012, 39(1).

[142] Geva A, Goldman A. Satisfaction measurement in guided tours. Annals of Tourism Research. 1991, 18(2).

[143] Hercbergs D. Narrating instability: political detouring in jerusalem. Mobilities. 2012, 7(3).

[144] Huang L, Kao P H. How to tell a good tour guide under different strategic orientations. African Journal of Business Management. 2011, 5(27).

[145] Huang S S, Hsu C H C, Chan A. Tour guide performance and tourist satisfaction: a study of the package tours in shanghai. Journal of Hospitality & Tourism Research. 2010, 34(1).

[146] Huang S S, Weiler B. A review and evaluation of China's quality assurance system for tour guiding. Journal of Sustainable Tourism. 2010, 18(7).

[147] Io M U, Hallo L. Tour guides' interpretation of the historic center of macao as a world cultural heritage site. Journal of Tourism and Cultural Change. 2011, 9(2).

[148] Jafari J. Special issue on tourist guides — pathfinders, mediators, and animators. Annals of Tourism Research. 1985(12).

[149] Jonasson M, Scherle N. Performing co-produced guided tours. Scandinavian Journal of Hospitality and Tourism. 2012, 12(1).

[150] Leclerc D, Martin J N. Tour guide communication competence: French, German and American tourists' perceptions. International Journal of Intercultural Relations. 2004, 28(3-4).

[151] Li X, Lai C T, Harrill R, Kline S, Wang L Y. When east meets west: An exploratory study on Chinese outbound tourists' travel expectations. Tourism Management. 2011, 32(4).

[152] Liao S K, Chen Y C, Chang K L, Tseng T W. Assessing the performance of Taiwanese tour guides. African Journal of Business Management. 2011, 5(4).

[153] Lin C T, Wang K C, Chen W Y. Female tour leaders as advertising endorsers. Service Industries Journal. 2008, 28(9).

[154] Lugosi P, Bray J. Tour guiding, organisational culture and learning: lessons from an entrepreneurial company. International Journal of Tourism Research. 2008, 10(5).

[155] Mak A H N, Wong K K F, Chang R C Y. Factors affecting the service quality of the tour guiding profession in Macau. International Journal of Tourism Research. 2010, 12(3).

[156] Min J C H. Tour guides' emotional intelligence in relation to demographic characteristics. African Journal of Business Management. 2010, 4(17).

[157] Min J C H. Tour guides and emotional intelligence. Annals of Tourism Research. 2011, 38(1).

[158] Mossberg L. Extraordinary experiences through storytelling. Scandinavian Journal of Hospitality and Tourism. 2008, 8(3).

[159] Overend D. Performing sites: illusion and authenticity in the spatial stories of the guided tour. Scandinavian Journal of Hospitality and Tourism. 2012, 12(1).

[160] Pearce P L. Tourist-guide interaction. Annals of Tourism Research. 1984, 11(1).

[161] Pereira E M, Mykletun R J. Guides as contributors to sustainable tourism? A case study from the amazon. Scandinavian Journal of Hospitality and Tourism.2012, 12(1).

[162] Randall C, Rollins R B. Visitor perceptions of the role of tour guides in natural areas. Journal of Sustainable Tourism. 2009, 17(3).

[163] Salazar N B. Tourism and glocalization — "Local" tour guiding. Annals of Tourism Research. 2005, 32(3).

[164] Salazar N B. Touristifying Tanzania — Local guides, global discourse. Annals of

Tourism Research. 2006, 33(3).

[165] Torres-Sovero C, Gonzalez J A, Martin-Lopez B, Kirkby C A. Social-ecological factors influencing tourist satisfaction in three ecotourism lodges in the southeastern Peruvian Amazon. Tourism Management. 2012, 33(3).

[166] Tsang N K F, Yeung S, Cheung C. A critical investigation of the use and effectiveness of interpretive services. Asia Pacific Journal of Tourism Research. 2011, 16(2).

[167] Wang K C, Hsieh A T, Chou S H, Lin Y S. GPTCCC: An instrument for measuring group package tour service. Tourism Management. 2007,28(2).

[168] Weiler B. Becoming a tour guide: The principles of guiding and site interpretation. Tourism Management. 2002, 23(2).

[169] Wong C U I, McKercher B. Day tour itineraries: Searching for the balance between commercial needs and experiential desires. Tourism Management. 2012, 33(6).

[170] Xu H G, Cui Q M, Ballantyne R, Packer J. Effective environmental interpretation at Chinese natural attractions: the need for an aesthetic approach. Journal of Sustainable Tourism. 2013, 21(1).

[171] Yamada N. Why tour guiding is important for ecotourism: enhancing guiding quality with the ecotourism promotion policy in japan. Asia Pacific Journal of Tourism Research. 2011, 16(2).

[172] Zhang H Q, Heung V C S, Yan Y Q. Play or not to play — An analysis of the mechanism of the zero-commission Chinese outbound tours through a game theory approach. Tourism Management. 2009, 30(3).

[173] Zillinger M, Jonasson M, Adolfsson P. Guided tours and tourism. Scandinavian Journal of Hospitality and Tourism. 2012, 12(1).

[174] http://www.world-tourism.org. World Tourism Organization, (世界旅游组织)

[175] http://www.wttc.org. World Travel and Tourism Council, (世界旅行与旅游协会)

[176] http://www.pata.org. Pacific Asia Travel Association, (亚太旅游协会)

[177] www.cnta.gov.cn. (中国国家旅游局)

[178] http://www.tourguide.net.cn. (中国导游网)

[179] http://www.wftga.org/, The World Federation of Tourist Guide Association, (世界导游协会)

[180] http://www.worldtourismfoundation.org/, The World Tourism Foundation, (世界旅游基金会)

[181] http://www.guidelondon.org.uk. The Association of Professional Tourist Guides, (英国执业导游协会)

[182] http://etoa.cvent.com. European Tour Operators Association, (欧洲导游协会)

[183] http://www.itg.org.uk. The Institute of Tourist Guiding, (英国导游学院)

[184] http://www.tmguk.com. The Travel Management Group, (英国旅游管理集团)

[185] http://www.britainsbestguides.org. The Guild of Registered Tourist Guides, (英国注册导游培训协会)

[186] http://www.bepaidtotravel.com. The International Guide Academy, Inc., (国际导游学院)
[187] http://www.tourmanager.org. International Association of Tour Managers, (国际旅行社经理协会)
[188] http://www.greenguidealliance.com. The Green Guide Alliance, (绿色导游联盟)
[189] http://www.ntaonline.com. The National Tour Association, (美国旅游协会)
[190] http://www.ustravel.org. The U.S. Travel Association, (美国旅行协会)
[191] http://www.ustoa.com. United States Tour Operators Association, (美国旅游社协会)
[192] http://www.tichk.org. The Travel Industry Council of Hong Kong, (香港旅游业协会)
[193] http://www.discoverhongkong.com. Hong Kong Tourism Board, (香港旅游发展局)

北京大学出版社本科旅游管理系列规划教材

序号	书　名	标准书号	主编	定价	出版时间	配套情况
1	旅游交通管理	7-301-25643-5	来逢波　陈松岩	31	2015	课件
2	会展节事策划与管理	7-301-25512-4	朱　华　张哲乐	35	2015	课件
3	酒店质量管理原理与实务	7-301-25543-8	张红卫　张　娓	37	2015	课件
4	旅游景区管理	7-301-25223-9	杨絮飞　蔡维英	39	2015	课件
5	旅游文化创意与策划	7-301-25166-9	徐兆寿	43	2015	课件
6	旅行社经营管理	7-301-25011-2	余志勇	35	2015	课件
7	现代酒店管理实用教程	7-301-24938-3	林　巧　张雪晶	38	2015	课件
8	旅游学概论	7-301-23875-2	朱　华	44	2014	课件
9	旅游心理学	7-301-23475-4	杨　娇	41	2014	课件
10	旅游法律法规教程	7-301-24850-8	魏　鹏	45	2014	课件、微课
11	旅游政策与法律法规	7-301-23697-0	李文汇　朱　华	43	2014	课件
12	旅游英语	7-301-23087-9	朱　华	48	2014	课件、光盘、视频
13	旅游企业战略管理	7-301-23604-8	王　慧	38	2014	课件
14	旅游文化学概论	7-301-23738-0	闫红霞　李玉华	37	2014	课件
15	西部民族民俗旅游	7-301-24383-1	欧阳正宇	54	2014	课件
16	休闲度假村经营与管理	7-301-24317-6	周绍健	40	2014	课件
17	会展业概论	7-301-23621-5	陈　楠	30	2014	课件
18	旅游学	7-301-22518-9	李　瑞	30	2013	课件
19	旅游学概论	7-301-21610-1	李玉华	42	2013	课件
20	旅游策划理论与实务	7-301-22630-8	李　锋　李　萌	43	2013	课件
21	景区经营与管理	7-301-23364-1	陈玉英	48	2013	课件
22	旅游资源开发与规划	7-301-22451-9	孟爱云	32	2013	课件
23	旅游地图编制与应用	7-301-23104-3	凌善金	38	2013	课件
24	旅游英语教程	7-301-22042-9	于立新	38	2013	课件
25	英语导游实务	7-301-22986-6	唐　勇	33	2013	课件
26	导游实务	7-301-22045-0	易婷婷	29	2013	课件
27	导游实务	7-301-21638-5	朱　斌	32	2013	课件
28	旅游服务礼仪	7-301-22940-8	徐兆寿	29	2013	课件
29	休闲学导论	7-301-22654-4	李经龙	30	2013	课件
30	休闲学导论	7-301-21655-2	吴文新	49	2013	课件
31	休闲活动策划与服务	7-301-22113-6	杨　梅	32	2013	课件
32	前厅客房服务与管理	7-301-22547-9	张青云	42	2013	课件
33	旅游学导论	7-301-21325-4	张金霞	36	2012	课件
34	旅游规划原理与实务	7-301-21221-9	郭　伟	35	2012	课件
35	旅游地形象设计学	7-301-20946-2	凌善金	30	2012	课件
36	旅游文化与传播	7-301-19349-5	潘文焰	38	2012	课件
37	旅游财务会计	7-301-20101-5	金莉芝	40	2012	课件
38	现代酒店管理与服务案例	7-301-17449-4	邢夫敏	29	2012	课件
39	餐饮运行与管理	7-301-21049-9	单铭磊	39	2012	课件
40	会展概论	7-301-21091-8	来逢波	33	2012	课件
41	旅行社门市管理实务	7-301-19339-6	梁雪松	39	2011	课件

如您需要更多教学资源如电子课件、电子样章、习题答案等，请登录北京大学出版社第六事业部官网 www.pup6.cn 搜索下载。

如您需要浏览更多专业教材，请扫下面的二维码，关注北京大学出版社第六事业部官方微信（微信号：pup6book），随时查询专业教材、浏览教材目录、内容简介等信息，并可在线申请纸质样书用于教学。

感谢您使用我们的教材，欢迎您随时与我们联系，我们将及时做好全方位的服务。联系方式：010-62750667，moyu333333@163.com，pup_6@163.com，lihu80@163.com，欢迎来电来信。客户服务QQ号：1292552107，欢迎随时咨询。